365 Days of Philosophy

A Year of Daily Lessons from the World's
Greatest Thinkers, from Socrates to Sartre —
130+ Philosophers on Life, Ethics, Stoicism,
Existentialism, and More

Dae Lee

airplane mode publishing house

Contents

Preface

In crafting "365 Days of Philosophy," our goal was to create a book that serves as both an introduction to philosophy and a daily source of inspiration. Each lesson is carefully curated to provide a balance of historical context, philosophical insight, and practical application. We believe that philosophy is not just an academic discipline but a way of life that can help us navigate the complexities of the modern world. All remaining errors are of course our own.

INTRODUCTION

Imagine having access to the wisdom of history's greatest minds, condensed into daily lessons that fit into your busy schedule. "365 Days of Philosophy" is your year-long guide to exploring the profound insights of more than 130 philosophers from around the globe, offering you a comprehensive journey through the world of thought. Each day, you'll uncover new perspectives and deepen your understanding of life's big questions, all without needing a formal philosophy degree.

Philosophy is often perceived as an esoteric field, but it fundamentally addresses questions that matter to everyone: What is reality? How should we live? What constitutes happiness? This book aims to demystify these questions, making philosophy accessible to all. By presenting complex ideas in daily, digestible lessons, we demonstrate that philosophy is not only relevant but essential to everyday life. Through the wisdom of over 130 philosophers, you'll find that philosophy can illuminate your understanding of the world and your place within it.

A key feature of this book is its chronological structure. Starting with the early pre-Socratic philosophers and moving through to contemporary thinkers, you will see the evolution of philosophical thought. This structure highlights the interconnectedness of ideas, showing how each philosopher builds upon the insights of their predecessors. By the end of the year, you will have a broad overview of Western philosophy, gaining a deep appreciation for the intellectual

1

legacy that continues to shape our world.

"365 Days of Philosophy" is not just a historical overview. It is designed to be practical and relevant to your daily life. Each lesson includes real-world examples and thought experiments to help you see the applicability of philosophical ideas. Whether you're facing ethical dilemmas at work, seeking personal growth, or curious about the nature of existence, you will find guidance and inspiration in these pages. Philosophy teaches us to think critically, live ethically, and understand deeply—skills that are invaluable in today's complex world.

Approach each lesson with an open mind and a reflective spirit. Consider the questions posed, engage with the thought experiments, and contemplate how these timeless ideas can enhance your life. Philosophy is not about finding definitive answers but about exploring the questions that define our human experience. Dive in and discover new perspectives, challenge your assumptions, and gain a deeper understanding of yourself and the world around you.

January 1: Thales of Miletus - Water as the Fundamental Substance

T HALES OF MILETUS, BORN around 624 BCE, is credited as the first philosopher in Western history. He
was one of the earliest figures to seek natural explanations
for the world's phenomena, moving away from mythological
narratives. Thales proposed that water is the fundamental
substance, or archê, of the universe. He observed that water
is essential for life, can exist in different states—liquid, solid
(as ice), and gas (as steam)—and hypothesized that all things
emerged from this singular, life-giving element.

Thales' assertion that water is the foundational element
was revolutionary for its time. He laid the groundwork for
future scientific inquiry by proposing a unified origin for
the diverse phenomena in the world. This was a significant
philosophical leap, suggesting that the complexity of the
universe could be understood through simpler, underlying
principles. His focus on water also reflected the importance
of observation and empirical evidence in forming explanations about the natural world, a departure from the supernatural explanations prevalent in his era.

Thales' influence extended beyond his specific claims about
water. He established a methodological precedent for later
philosophers and scientists: seeking natural, rather than
supernatural, explanations for natural events. By identifying
water as the common denominator in all matter, Thales also
hinted at the idea of a unifying element in nature, a concept
that would inspire subsequent philosophers in their quest
to understand the cosmos. His work marked a foundational
moment in the history of philosophy and natural science.

January 2: Thales of Miletus - Prediction of Solar Eclipses

T HALES OF MILETUS WAS not only a philosopher but also an accomplished astronomer and mathematician. One of his most notable achievements was predicting a solar eclipse that occurred on May 28, 585 BCE. This event is significant because it demonstrated the potential of human reason and observation to understand and predict celestial phenomena. Thales' successful prediction marked a turning point in the history of science, showcasing the power of empirical observation and logical reasoning.

The ability to predict solar eclipses required a deep understanding of the movements of celestial bodies. Thales' work in this area laid the groundwork for future developments in astronomy and mathematics. His methods likely involved careful observations of the patterns and cycles of the sun and moon, combined with mathematical calculations. By moving away from mythological explanations and towards scientific methods, Thales exemplified the potential of human intellect to unlock the mysteries of the cosmos.

This achievement is a reminder of the importance of observation and critical thinking in our own lives. Thales' approach encourages us to look beyond immediate appearances and seek deeper explanations for the phenomena we encounter. Whether in science, philosophy, or everyday problem-solving, the principles of careful observation and logical reasoning that Thales championed remain vital tools for understanding and navigating the world.

January 3: Thales of Miletus - Earth Floats on Water

I N ADDITION TO HIS groundbreaking work on the fundamental substance of the universe and his astronomical achievements, Thales of Miletus also proposed that the Earth floats on water. This idea, while scientifically inaccurate by modern standards, was an early attempt to explain the stability of the Earth and the occurrence of natural phenomena such as earthquakes. Thales' hypothesis that the Earth rests on a vast body of water illustrates his effort to provide a naturalistic explanation for the world around him.

Thales' belief that the Earth floats on water reflects the broader context of early Greek cosmology, which sought to understand the structure and dynamics of the world through observation and reasoning. This idea is significant because it represents an early move towards scientific explanations, moving away from mythological interpretations. Thales' work laid the foundation for later philosophers and scientists who would continue to explore and refine our understanding of the natural world.

Despite its inaccuracies, Thales' hypothesis encourages us to think creatively and to question the status quo. It reminds us that the pursuit of knowledge often involves trial and error and that even incorrect theories can pave the way for future discoveries. Thales' legacy lies in his willingness to ask bold questions and seek rational explanations, a spirit of inquiry that continues to drive scientific and philosophical advancements today.

JANUARY 4: ANAXIMANDER - THE INFINITE (APEIRON) AS THE ORIGIN

A NAXIMANDER, A STUDENT OF Thales and a prominent pre-Socratic philosopher, introduced the concept
of the "apeiron," an indefinite and boundless principle. He
proposed that this infinite substance, rather than any specific material element, is the source of all things. Anaximander's apeiron is not a tangible substance like water or air but
an abstract, limitless entity from which the cosmos emerges
and into which it eventually dissolves.

Anaximander's theory of the apeiron reflects his understanding of the universe as governed by cycles of generation
and destruction, with all things returning to this primordial
source. This idea challenged the more concrete notions of
his predecessors and contributed to a more abstract conception of the origins of the cosmos. The apeiron ensured the
balance of opposites, such as hot and cold or wet and dry,
by providing a foundation that transcends physical distinctions.

Anaximander's contributions significantly influenced the
development of metaphysical thought, encouraging future
philosophers to consider non-material origins and the principles governing existence. His work represents a crucial
step in the transition from mythological to rational explanations of the universe.

JANUARY 5: ANAXIMANDER - EVOLUTIONARY THEORY OF LIFE

A NAXIMANDER IS ALSO CREDITED with developing one of the earliest evolutionary theories of life. He proposed that life originated in the moist environment of the early Earth and that the first living creatures were born in water. Anaximander believed that humans and other land-dwelling animals evolved from these aquatic beings, adapting to their environments over time. This idea was groundbreaking, as it suggested a natural process of development and adaptation long before the modern theory of evolution was formulated.

Anaximander's evolutionary theory of life reflects his broader philosophical inquiry into the origins and development of the natural world. By proposing that life evolved from simpler forms, Anaximander challenged the conventional belief that species were fixed and unchanging. His ideas laid the groundwork for future thinkers who would explore the processes of natural selection and adaptation, ultimately leading to the development of modern evolutionary biology.

The significance of Anaximander's evolutionary theory lies in its emphasis on natural processes and the dynamic nature of life. His work encourages us to consider how living organisms adapt and evolve in response to their environments, a concept that remains central to our understanding of biology. Anaximander's contributions remind us of the importance of looking at the natural world through a lens of change and development, inspiring ongoing exploration and discovery.

January 6: Anaximander - Earth is Free-Floating in Space

A NAXIMANDER'S COSMOLOGICAL VIEWS WERE also ahead of his time. He proposed that the Earth is free-floating in space, unsupported by anything, and that it remains in its position due to a state of equilibrium. This idea was a significant departure from the traditional view that the Earth was supported by a physical structure, such as water or a giant creature. Anaximander's hypothesis that the Earth floats freely in space reflects his innovative thinking and his willingness to challenge established cosmological models.

The concept of a free-floating Earth suggests a universe governed by natural laws and forces rather than by mythological or supernatural explanations. Anaximander's idea of equilibrium implies that the Earth's position is maintained by a balance of forces, a notion that aligns with modern scientific principles of gravity and motion. His cosmological views paved the way for later philosophers and scientists who would continue to explore and refine our understanding of the structure and dynamics of the cosmos.

Anaximander's belief in a free-floating Earth encourages us to think critically about the nature of our universe and the forces that govern it. His work exemplifies the importance of questioning established ideas and seeking rational explanations for natural phenomena. Anaximander's legacy lies in his ability to imagine a world governed by natural principles, inspiring future generations of thinkers to explore the mysteries of the cosmos through observation and reasoning.

JANUARY 7: LAOZI - WU WEI: EFFORTLESS ACTION

L AOZI, AN ANCIENT CHINESE philosopher and the re-
puted author of the Dao De Jing, was born around the
6th century BCE. He is best known for founding Daoism, a
philosophical and spiritual tradition that emphasizes living
in harmony with the Dao, or the fundamental principle that
underlies everything in the universe. One of Laozi's core
teachings is the concept of "wu wei," which translates to
"effortless action" or "non-action." Wu wei encourages individuals to align with the natural flow of the Dao, acting in
a way that is spontaneous and unforced.

The principle of wu wei suggests that by following the natural course of events and minimizing unnecessary effort,
one can achieve a state of harmony and balance. Laozi believed that forcing actions or striving too hard against the
natural order leads to stress and disharmony. Instead, he
advocated for a way of life that is in tune with the rhythms
of nature, where actions are performed effortlessly and outcomes are achieved naturally.

Laozi's teaching of wu wei offers a powerful lesson for modern life, reminding us of the importance of balance and
the benefits of going with the flow. In a world that often
emphasizes relentless pursuit and constant effort, wu wei
provides a counterpoint, encouraging us to find harmony by
aligning our actions with the natural order. This approach
can lead to greater peace, efficiency, and satisfaction in both
our personal and professional lives.

January 8: Laozi - The Dao as the Fundamental Principle

A T THE HEART OF Laozi's philosophy is the concept of the Dao, which he describes as the ultimate, unnameable source of all existence. The Dao is both the origin and the underlying order of the universe, guiding the natural flow of all things. Unlike other philosophical traditions that seek to define or categorize the ultimate reality, Laozi emphasizes the ineffable nature of the Dao, suggesting that it cannot be fully understood or expressed through language.

Laozi's description of the Dao highlights the interconnectedness of all things and the cyclical patterns of nature. He teaches that everything in the universe is a manifestation of the Dao and that by understanding and aligning with this fundamental principle, one can achieve a state of harmony and balance. The Dao is seen as both the source and the sustainer of life, guiding the natural processes of growth, decay, and renewal.

The concept of the Dao invites us to contemplate the deeper, often mysterious forces that shape our lives and the world around us. Laozi's teachings encourage us to recognize the limitations of human understanding and to embrace the wisdom of humility and openness. By attuning ourselves to the Dao, we can find a sense of peace and purpose, trusting in the natural flow of the universe to guide our actions and decisions.

January 9: Laozi - Simplicity in Living

L AOZI'S PHILOSOPHY PLACES A strong emphasis on simplicity and contentment as keys to a fulfilling life. He advocates for a lifestyle that is free from excessive desires and materialism, encouraging individuals to appreciate the simple pleasures and natural beauty of the world. Laozi's teachings suggest that true happiness and tranquility come from living in accordance with the Dao, rather than pursuing wealth, power, or social status.

The Dao De Jing, Laozi's foundational text, contains numerous passages that extol the virtues of simplicity, humility, and contentment. Laozi warns against the dangers of greed and ambition, arguing that they lead to conflict and disharmony. Instead, he promotes a way of life that values modesty, frugality, and a deep connection with nature. By simplifying our lives and focusing on what truly matters, we can achieve a state of inner peace and balance.

Laozi's emphasis on simplicity offers a timeless lesson in a world often driven by consumerism and the constant pursuit of more. His teachings remind us that happiness is not found in external possessions or achievements but in a harmonious relationship with ourselves and the natural world. By embracing simplicity and aligning with the Dao, we can cultivate a life of contentment, mindfulness, and genuine fulfillment.

January 10: Anaximenes - Air as the Fundamental Substance

A NAXIMENES, A NOTABLE PRE-SOCRATIC philosopher, argued that air is the fundamental substance from which all things originate. Unlike Thales, who proposed water as the basic element, Anaximenes believed air's capacity for transformation was key to understanding the diversity of the natural world. He posited that air could become denser or rarer through processes such as condensation and rarefaction, respectively, leading to the formation of other substances. For example, through rarefaction, air becomes fire, while through condensation, it transforms into water and eventually earth.

Anaximenes' theory was based on empirical observations. He noted everyday phenomena, such as how breath condenses on a cold surface to form droplets or how air flows to create wind, to support his argument. By suggesting that a single substance could change into different forms, he introduced a proto-scientific method of explaining natural phenomena. This marked a significant departure from mythological explanations and aligned more closely with what would become the scientific approach: seeking natural causes for natural events.

The idea that air is the fundamental substance contributed to early notions of matter and change. Anaximenes' emphasis on a single, underlying principle influencing all matter laid a foundational concept in philosophy and natural science. His work influenced subsequent thinkers by encouraging the search for a common origin of all things and by framing the natural world as an interconnected system.

January 11: Anaximenes - Processes of Condensation and Rarefaction

B UILDING ON HIS IDEA that air is the fundamental substance, Anaximenes introduced the processes of condensation and rarefaction to explain the transformation of matter. He observed that when air condenses, it becomes visible and tangible, like clouds, water, and eventually earth. Conversely, when air rarefies, it becomes fire. This early form of the scientific method – observing natural phenomena to draw conclusions – set the stage for future scientific inquiry. By considering how air changes form, Anaximenes provided a framework for understanding the physical world's dynamic nature.

In our daily lives, the principles of condensation and rarefaction can be metaphorically applied to our thoughts and emotions. When we allow our thoughts to condense, focusing them into specific, actionable ideas, we can achieve tangible results. On the other hand, when we let our thoughts rarefy, we can access creativity and new perspectives. Balancing these processes can lead to a more harmonious and productive mindset, much like the balance in nature that Anaximenes observed.

Understanding these processes can also enhance our approach to problem-solving. Condensation represents narrowing down options to find practical solutions, while rarefaction involves broadening our perspective to consider innovative possibilities. By alternating between these states, we can tackle challenges more effectively, ensuring that our solutions are both practical and imaginative. Anaximenes' insights remind us of the value in both focusing and expanding our thinking to navigate life's complexities.

JANUARY 12: ANAXIMENES - INFINITE UNIVERSE

A NAXIMENES ALSO SPECULATED ABOUT the infinite nature of the universe. Unlike some of his contemporaries who believed in a finite cosmos, Anaximenes envisioned a boundless universe, where air extended infinitely in all directions. This idea of an infinite universe was groundbreaking, pushing the boundaries of how people understood their place in the cosmos. It challenged the notion of a limited, enclosed world, opening up the possibility of endless exploration and discovery.

This concept can be incredibly liberating in our personal lives. Embracing the idea of an infinite universe can inspire us to think beyond our perceived limitations and explore new possibilities. It encourages a mindset of growth and endless potential, reminding us that there is always more to learn, discover, and achieve. This perspective can be particularly empowering when faced with challenges, as it suggests that solutions and opportunities are boundless.

Anaximenes' vision of an infinite universe also has philosophical implications for our understanding of life and existence. It invites us to consider the endless possibilities that lie beyond our immediate experience and to approach life with a sense of curiosity and wonder. By viewing the world through the lens of infinity, we can cultivate a deeper appreciation for the mysteries and expansiveness of the universe, fostering a sense of awe and continuous learning.

JANUARY 13: PYTHAGORAS - THE IMPORTANCE OF NUMBERS

P YTHAGORAS, AN ANCIENT GREEK philosopher and mathematician, believed that numbers were the essence of all things. He posited that the universe is governed by mathematical relationships, and understanding these relationships reveals the underlying harmony of existence. Pythagoras and his followers, the Pythagoreans, discovered that numbers and mathematical ratios could explain musical harmony, celestial movements, and even ethical behavior. This mathematical worldview suggests that everything in the universe is interconnected through numerical patterns.

In practical terms, Pythagoras' emphasis on numbers encourages us to recognize the patterns and structures in our lives. From budgeting and planning to analyzing trends and making data-driven decisions, appreciating the importance of numbers can lead to more informed and effective choices. It also highlights the value of precision and clarity, urging us to approach problems systematically and logically.

Moreover, Pythagoras' insights can enhance our appreciation of beauty and order in the world. By recognizing the mathematical principles underlying art, music, and nature, we can develop a deeper understanding and appreciation of the world around us. This perspective encourages us to look beyond the surface and see the intricate patterns that shape our reality, fostering a sense of wonder and respect for the natural order.

January 14: Pythagoras - Transmigration of Souls

O NE OF PYTHAGORAS' MOST intriguing teachings is the doctrine of transmigration of souls, or metempsychosis. He believed that souls are immortal and, upon death, move into a new body, whether human or animal. This cycle of rebirth continues until the soul achieves purification and liberation. This belief influenced not only Pythagorean philosophy but also later religious and philosophical traditions, including Plato's theories and certain Eastern philosophies.

The concept of transmigration can serve as a powerful metaphor for personal growth and transformation. It suggests that we are not bound by our past and that we have the potential to change and evolve continuously. This perspective encourages us to view challenges and setbacks as opportunities for learning and growth, rather than as permanent failures. It fosters a mindset of resilience and adaptability, empowering us to navigate life's ups and downs with grace.

Additionally, the idea of transmigration invites us to consider the interconnectedness of all life. By recognizing that every being may contain a soul on its journey towards purification, we can cultivate compassion and empathy for others. This perspective encourages us to treat all living things with kindness and respect, acknowledging our shared journey towards self-improvement and enlightenment.

JANUARY 15: PYTHAGORAS - HARMONY OF THE SPHERES

P YTHAGORAS ALSO INTRODUCED THE concept of the Harmony of the Spheres, which posits that celestial bodies move according to mathematical equations, producing a symphony of music that is inaudible to the human ear. This idea reflects Pythagoras' belief in a harmonious and ordered universe, governed by mathematical principles. The Harmony of the Spheres suggests that the cosmos operates like a well-tuned instrument, with each part contributing to the overall harmony.

This concept can be applied to our daily lives by encouraging us to seek harmony and balance in our own endeavors. Just as the planets move in a coordinated and harmonious manner, we can strive to align our actions and goals with our values and principles. This alignment can lead to a more fulfilling and balanced life, where our efforts contribute to a greater sense of purpose and well-being.

The Harmony of the Spheres also underscores the importance of interconnectedness and cooperation. In a harmonious system, each component plays a crucial role in maintaining balance and order. Similarly, in our personal and professional relationships, recognizing and valuing each individual's contribution can lead to more effective and harmonious collaborations. By striving for harmony in our interactions and endeavors, we can create a more cohesive and supportive environment.

January 16: Confucius - The Importance of Moral Integrity (Ren)

CONFUCIUS, A RENOWNED CHINESE philosopher, emphasized the importance of moral integrity, or "ren" (仁), as the foundation of a virtuous life. Ren, often translated as "benevolence" or "humaneness," represents the highest ethical standard, guiding one's actions and interactions. Confucius believed that cultivating ren leads to personal and societal harmony, as individuals strive to act with kindness, empathy, and respect towards others.

In practical terms, embracing ren means prioritizing ethical behavior in all aspects of life. This involves treating others with compassion, fairness, and respect, and making decisions that align with moral principles. By practicing ren, we can build stronger, more positive relationships and contribute to a more just and harmonious society. It also encourages us to reflect on our actions and strive for continuous self-improvement, fostering a sense of moral responsibility and integrity.

Ren can also enhance our personal well-being by promoting a sense of inner peace and fulfillment. Acting with kindness and empathy not only benefits others but also nurtures our own emotional health. By cultivating ren, we can develop a more positive and compassionate outlook on life, leading to greater happiness and contentment. This principle reminds us that true success and fulfillment come from living a life of integrity and virtue.

JANUARY 17: CONFUCIUS - PROPER CONDUCT THROUGH RITUAL (LI)

C ONFUCIUS ALSO EMPHASIZED THE importance of "li" (⬚), or proper conduct through ritual. Li encompasses not only formal rituals and ceremonies but also everyday manners and behaviors that promote social harmony. Confucius believed that adhering to li helps individuals cultivate self-discipline and respect for others, creating a structured and harmonious society. By following established norms and customs, people can navigate social interactions more effectively and maintain order and stability.

In our modern lives, the concept of li can be applied to the way we interact with others and adhere to social norms. Practicing good manners, showing respect for cultural traditions, and observing social etiquette can enhance our relationships and create a more harmonious community. Li encourages us to be mindful of our actions and their impact on others, fostering a sense of responsibility and mutual respect.

Moreover, li can help us develop self-discipline and personal growth. By adhering to established routines and practices, we can cultivate a sense of order and consistency in our lives. This discipline can extend to various areas, such as work, health, and personal development, leading to greater productivity and well-being. Confucius' emphasis on li reminds us of the value of structure and tradition in creating a balanced and harmonious life.

JANUARY 18: CONFUCIUS - FILIAL PIETY AS THE FOUNDATION OF SOCIETY

FILIAL PIETY, OR "XIAO" (⊠), is another central tenet of Confucius' philosophy. Xiao refers to the respect and devotion that children owe to their parents and ancestors. Confucius believed that filial piety is the foundation of a stable and harmonious society, as it fosters strong family bonds and a sense of duty and respect. By honoring their parents and ancestors, individuals learn to cultivate similar virtues in their interactions with others, contributing to social harmony and stability.

In practical terms, practicing filial piety involves showing respect and gratitude towards our parents and elders. This can include providing care and support, expressing appreciation, and up holding family traditions and values. By honoring our familial relationships, we can strengthen our family bonds and create a supportive and loving environment. Filial piety also teaches us the importance of gratitude and respect, which can extend to our interactions with others.

Filial piety can also enhance our personal growth and character development. By cultivating a sense of duty and responsibility towards our family, we learn to prioritize others' well-being and develop empathy and compassion. This sense of duty can inspire us to act with integrity and kindness in all aspects of life, leading to a more fulfilling and meaningful existence. Confucius' emphasis on xiao reminds us of the importance of family and the enduring impact of our relationships on personal and societal well-being.

January 19: Heraclitus - Change is the Only Constant (Panta Rhei)

H ERACLITUS, AN ANCIENT GREEK philosopher, is best known for his doctrine that "change is the only constant" (panta rhei). He believed that everything in the universe is in a state of flux, and nothing remains the same. Heraclitus famously stated that one cannot step into the same river twice, as the water is constantly flowing and changing. This perspective highlights the transient nature of existence and the inevitability of change.

In practical terms, embracing Heraclitus' philosophy can help us navigate the uncertainties and challenges of life. By accepting that change is a natural and unavoidable part of existence, we can develop resilience and adaptability. This mindset encourages us to be open to new experiences, learn from our mistakes, and continuously evolve. Embracing change can also reduce our fear of the unknown and help us approach life with a sense of curiosity and wonder.

Heraclitus' insights can also enhance our personal growth and development. Recognizing that change is constant can inspire us to pursue continuous self-improvement and embrace lifelong learning. It encourages us to view challenges and setbacks as opportunities for growth and transformation, rather than as obstacles. By adopting a flexible and adaptive approach to life, we can navigate its complexities more effectively and cultivate a sense of inner strength and resilience.

January 20: Heraclitus - Unity of Opposites

H ERACLITUS ALSO INTRODUCED THE concept of the unity of opposites, positing that seemingly contradictory forces are interconnected and interdependent. He believed that opposites, such as hot and cold, light and dark, and life and death, exist in a state of dynamic tension, creating balance and harmony in the universe. This idea suggests that conflict and contrast are essential for growth and transformation, as they drive the continuous process of change.

In practical terms, embracing the unity of opposites can help us navigate life's complexities and contradictions. By recognizing that opposing forces are interconnected, we can develop a more nuanced and balanced perspective. This mindset encourages us to appreciate the value of diversity and contrast, fostering a greater sense of empathy and understanding. It also helps us to see challenges and conflicts as opportunities for growth and learning, rather than as sources of stress and frustration.

The unity of opposites can also enhance our personal relationships and interactions. By recognizing the interconnectedness of opposing viewpoints, we can develop greater tolerance and open-mindedness. This perspective encourages us to seek common ground and appreciate the value of different perspectives, leading to more harmonious and constructive interactions. Heraclitus' insights remind us of the importance of balance and harmony in navigating the complexities of life and relationships.

January 21: Heraclitus - Logos as the Rational Principle

H ERACLITUS INTRODUCED THE CONCEPT of "logos" as the rational principle governing the universe. He believed that logos is the underlying order and reason that guides the continuous process of change. While everything is in flux, logos provides a coherent and rational structure to the universe, ensuring that change occurs in an ordered and predictable manner. Heraclitus' concept of logos highlights the importance of reason and rationality in understanding and navigating the world.

In practical terms, embracing the concept of logos encourages us to cultivate rationality and critical thinking in our daily lives. By applying reason and logic to our decisions and actions, we can make more informed and effective choices. This approach helps us to navigate complex situations and challenges with greater clarity and confidence. It also encourages us to seek knowledge and understanding, fostering a sense of curiosity and intellectual growth.

The concept of logos can also enhance our personal development and well-being. By cultivating a rational and balanced mindset, we can approach life's challenges with greater resilience and equanimity. This perspective helps us to manage our emotions and reactions more effectively, reducing stress and promoting a sense of inner peace. Heraclitus' emphasis on logos reminds us of the value of reason and rationality in navigating the complexities of life and achieving personal fulfillment.

JANUARY 22: PARMENIDES - REALITY IS UNCHANGING AND INDIVISIBLE

P ARMENIDES, AN ANCIENT GREEK philosopher, introduced the idea that reality is unchanging and indivisible. Unlike Heraclitus, who emphasized constant change,
Parmenides argued that change is an illusion. He believed
that true being is eternal, uniform, and unalterable. For Parmenides, the sensory world, with its perceived changes and
diversity, is deceptive; only through reason can one grasp
the truth of an unchanging reality.

This perspective can profoundly impact our understanding
of stability in our lives. In a world that feels increasingly
chaotic, embracing Parmenides' idea can provide a sense of
constancy and peace. By focusing on the enduring aspects
of our existence - such as values, relationships, and inner
truths - we can find stability amidst external changes. It
encourages us to look beyond surface appearances and connect with deeper, unchanging principles.

Moreover, Parmenides' philosophy invites us to question
our perceptions and rely on reason. It challenges us to distinguish between what is real and what is merely an illusion, fostering critical thinking and deeper insight. This
approach can be applied to various aspects of life, from
personal relationships to professional endeavors, helping us
make more informed and rational decisions.

JANUARY 23: PARMENIDES - THE WAY OF TRUTH AND THE WAY OF OPINION

P ARMENIDES DISTINGUISHED BETWEEN TWO paths of understanding: the Way of Truth and the Way of Opinion. The Way of Truth, he argued, is the path of reason and logic, leading to the understanding that reality is one, unchanging, and eternal. The Way of Opinion, on the other hand, is based on sensory perception and leads to the false belief in change and multiplicity. Parmenides urged individuals to follow the Way of Truth to achieve genuine knowledge.

In our daily lives, this distinction encourages us to prioritize rational thought over fleeting impressions. It suggests that we should seek knowledge through careful reasoning rather than relying solely on our senses or opinions shaped by external influences. This approach can help us navigate complex situations with greater clarity and discernment, allowing us to uncover deeper truths.

Additionally, Parmenides' emphasis on the Way of Truth highlights the importance of intellectual integrity. By committing to rigorous reasoning and avoiding superficial judgments, we can cultivate a more thoughtful and authentic understanding of the world. This mindset fosters intellectual growth and encourages a lifelong pursuit of wisdom.

January 24: Parmenides - Being is Eternal and Unchanging

P ARMENIDES' CENTRAL TENET IS that being is eternal and unchanging. He posited that what truly exists cannot come into being or perish, as this would imply change, which he deemed impossible. For Parmenides, true being is timeless, uniform, and indivisible, standing in stark contrast to the changing, transient world perceived by our senses.

This concept can be comforting in the face of life's uncertainties. It suggests that beneath the surface of constant change, there is an eternal, stable reality. Embracing this idea can help us cultivate a sense of inner peace and resilience, knowing that while circumstances may change, certain fundamental truths remain constant.

Furthermore, Parmenides' philosophy encourages us to seek out and connect with these enduring aspects of existence. By focusing on timeless values and principles, we can navigate life's challenges with greater confidence and stability. This perspective can also inspire us to contribute to something lasting and meaningful, fostering a sense of purpose and fulfillment.

January 25: Protagoras - Man is the Measure of All Things

P ROTAGORAS, A PREEMINENT SOPHIST and Greek philosopher, is famous for his assertion that "man is the measure of all things." This means that individual perception is the ultimate standard of truth, implying that what is true for one person may not be true for another. Protagoras championed the idea that knowledge is subjective and that each person's perspective is valid.

In practical terms, Protagoras' philosophy encourages us to respect diverse viewpoints and experiences. It suggests that truth can vary based on individual perceptions, promoting tolerance and open-mindedness. This approach can enhance our interpersonal relationships by fostering empathy and understanding, allowing us to appreciate others' perspectives even when they differ from our own.

Moreover, recognizing the subjective nature of knowledge can empower us to take ownership of our beliefs and experiences. It encourages us to reflect on our perceptions and consider how they shape our understanding of the world. This introspection can lead to greater self-awareness and personal growth, as we explore the unique lens through which we view life.

January 26: Protagoras - Relativism

P ROTAGORAS IS ALSO KNOWN for his advocacy of relativism, the idea that there are no absolute truths and that truth is relative to the individual or culture. He argued that beliefs and values are shaped by cultural and personal contexts, and therefore, what is considered true or right can vary widely. This perspective challenges the notion of universal standards and highlights the diversity of human thought and experience.

In our modern world, embracing relativism can foster greater cultural sensitivity and inclusivity. It encourages us to recognize and respect the varied beliefs and practices of different cultures, promoting a more harmonious and interconnected global community. This approach can also help us navigate moral and ethical dilemmas by considering the context and perspectives involved.

Relativism also invites us to be more flexible and adaptable in our thinking. By acknowledging that our own beliefs are shaped by our experiences and context, we can remain open to new ideas and perspectives. This openness can enhance our problem-solving abilities and creativity, as we draw on a broader range of insights and approaches.

January 27: Protagoras - Agnosticism about the Gods

P ROTAGORAS FAMOUSLY DECLARED AGNOSTICISM regarding the existence of gods, stating, "Concerning the gods, I have no means of knowing whether they exist or not, nor of what sort they may be." This statement reflects his broader skepticism and emphasizes the limits of human knowledge. Protagoras suggested that certain questions, particularly those concerning the divine, may be beyond our capacity to answer definitively.

This agnostic perspective can encourage intellectual humility and open-mindedness. By acknowledging the limits of our knowledge, we can approach complex questions with curiosity and a willingness to explore multiple possibilities. This mindset can foster a more thoughtful and reflective approach to life, as we remain open to new insights and understandings.

Protagoras' agnosticism also highlights the importance of critical thinking and skepticism. It encourages us to question assumptions and seek evidence, rather than accepting claims at face value. This approach can enhance our decision-making and problem-solving skills, as we evaluate information more rigorously and thoughtfully.

JANUARY 28: MOZI - UNIVERSAL LOVE (JIAN AI)

M OZI, AN INFLUENTIAL CHINESE philosopher, advocated for the principle of "jian ai" or universal love. He believed that all people should care for each other equally, regardless of their relationship or status. This principle stands in contrast to Confucianism, which emphasizes hierarchical relationships and familial loyalty. Mozi argued that universal love leads to social harmony and reduces conflict, as people act with compassion and fairness towards all.

In practical terms, embracing universal love encourages us to extend kindness and empathy beyond our immediate circles. It challenges us to treat everyone with respect and consideration, fostering a more inclusive and compassionate society. This approach can enhance our personal relationships and contribute to a more supportive and connected community.

Moreover, Mozi's principle of universal love can inspire us to engage in acts of altruism and social justice. By advocating for the well-being of others, we can contribute to positive change and address social inequalities. This perspective encourages us to think beyond our own interests and consider the broader impact of our actions, fostering a sense of global responsibility and interconnectedness.

January 29: Mozi - Opposition to Fatalism

M OZI STRONGLY OPPOSED FATALISM, the belief that events are predetermined and inevitable. He argued that such beliefs lead to passivity and inaction, as people resign themselves to their fate rather than striving to improve their circumstances. Mozi believed in the power of human agency and the ability to shape one's destiny through effort and ethical behavior. He emphasized the importance of proactive problem-solving and personal responsibility.

This anti-fatalistic stance can empower us to take control of our lives and strive for positive change. By rejecting the notion that our futures are predetermined, we can embrace a sense of agency and accountability. This mindset encourages us to set goals, work towards them, and persevere in the face of challenges, fostering resilience and determination.

Furthermore, Mozi's opposition to fatalism highlights the value of ethical behavior and social responsibility. It suggests that our actions can make a meaningful difference in the world, inspiring us to contribute positively to our communities and society. This perspective promotes a proactive and engaged approach to life, where we actively seek to create a better future for ourselves and others.

JANUARY 30: MOZI - PRACTICAL BENEFITS AND UTILITARIANISM

M OZI WAS AN EARLY advocate of utilitarianism, the ethical theory that actions should be judged based on their practical benefits and overall utility. He believed that policies and behaviors should be evaluated by their ability to promote the greatest good for the greatest number. This pragmatic approach to ethics emphasizes outcomes and the tangible impact of actions, rather than intentions or abstract principles.

In our daily lives, adopting a utilitarian perspective can help us make more effective and beneficial decisions. By considering the practical consequences of our actions, we can prioritize choices that maximize positive outcomes and minimize harm. This approach encourages a results-oriented mindset, where we focus on the tangible benefits of our actions for ourselves and others.

Mozi's utilitarianism also underscores the importance of social welfare and collective well-being. It inspires us to consider the broader impact of our decisions and to act in ways that contribute to the common good. This perspective can enhance our sense of social responsibility and encourage us to support policies and initiatives that promote fairness, equity, and overall societal benefit.

January 31: Socrates - Know Thyself

S OCRATES, ONE OF THE most influential philosophers in Western history, famously emphasized the importance of self-knowledge with the maxim "Know thyself." He believed that true wisdom comes from understanding oneself – one's values, motivations, strengths, and weaknesses. For Socrates, self-knowledge was the foundation of ethical behavior and personal growth, as it enables individuals to live authentic and virtuous lives.

In practical terms, embracing self-knowledge encourages us to engage in introspection and self-reflection. By regularly examining our thoughts, actions, and motivations, we can develop a deeper understanding of ourselves and our place in the world. This self-awareness can guide our decisions and actions, helping us to align them with our values and aspirations.

Furthermore, Socrates' emphasis on self-knowledge highlights the importance of lifelong learning and personal growth. It suggests that wisdom is not a fixed state but an ongoing process of discovery and development. This perspective encourages us to remain curious and open to new experiences, continually seeking to understand ourselves and the world more deeply.

FEBRUARY 1: SOCRATES - THE SOCRATIC METHOD

S OCRATES IS ALSO RENOWNED for developing the Socratic Method, a form of cooperative dialogue aimed at stimulating critical thinking and illuminating ideas. This method involves asking a series of probing questions to challenge assumptions, clarify concepts, and uncover underlying beliefs. Socrates used this approach to engage others in deep philosophical discussions, fostering an environment of inquiry and intellectual rigor.

In practical terms, the Socratic Method can enhance our problem-solving and decision-making skills. By asking thoughtful questions and examining our assumptions, we can gain a clearer understanding of complex issues and develop more effective solutions. This approach encourages us to think critically and analytically, fostering a mindset of curiosity and open-mindedness.

Moreover, the Socratic Method can improve our communication and interpersonal skills. By engaging others in meaningful dialogue and actively listening to their perspectives, we can build stronger, more collaborative relationships. This approach promotes mutual understanding and respect, creating a more supportive and intellectually stimulating environment.

FEBRUARY 2: SOCRATES - ETHICS OVER WEALTH

S OCRATES FAMOUSLY PRIORITIZED ETHICS and virtue over wealth and material success. He believed that true happiness and fulfillment come from living a virtuous life, guided by principles of justice, integrity, and wisdom. For Socrates, the pursuit of wealth and power was secondary to the cultivation of moral character and the pursuit of knowledge. He often challenged his contemporaries to reflect on their values and consider the ethical implications of their actions.

In practical terms, Socrates' emphasis on ethics over wealth encourages us to prioritize our values and principles in our daily lives. It suggests that true success and fulfillment come from living with integrity and aligning our actions with our beliefs. This perspective can help us navigate ethical dilemmas and make decisions that reflect our highest ideals, fostering a sense of inner peace and satisfaction.

Furthermore, Socrates' philosophy invites us to reconsider our definitions of success and happiness. By focusing on personal growth, meaningful relationships, and contributions to the common good, we can cultivate a deeper sense of purpose and well-being. This approach challenges the materialistic values prevalent in modern society, encouraging us to seek fulfillment through ethical living and the pursuit of wisdom.

FEBRUARY 3: PLATO - THE THEORY OF FORMS

P LATO, ONE OF THE most influential figures in Western philosophy, introduced the Theory of Forms. According to Plato, the material world we perceive through our senses is not the true reality. Instead, it is a shadow of a higher, unchanging reality called the Forms or Ideas. For instance, while there are many individual chairs, they all share the Form of "Chairness," which is the perfect, immutable essence of what a chair is.

Plato used the example of geometry to illustrate his point. When we think of a perfect circle, it exists only as an idea because no physical circle can be perfectly round. The Form of a circle represents this perfect ideal. Plato argued that true knowledge comes from understanding these Forms, not just observing their imperfect copies in the material world.

This distinction between the world of appearances and the world of Forms suggests that we must use reason and philosophical inquiry to grasp the true nature of reality. Plato's Theory of Forms laid the groundwork for his later philosophical explorations and influenced countless thinkers in the Western philosophical tradition.

FEBRUARY 4: PLATO - THE ALLEGORY OF THE CAVE

IN "THE REPUBLIC," PLATO presents the Allegory of the Cave to illustrate his theory of knowledge and enlightenment. In the allegory, prisoners are chained inside a dark cave, facing a wall. Behind them is a fire, and between the fire and the prisoners are objects being moved by unseen handlers, casting shadows on the wall. The prisoners take these shadows to be the only reality.

One prisoner is freed and discovers the outside world, realizing that the shadows were mere illusions. He sees the sun, which represents the Form of the Good, the ultimate source of truth and knowledge. Upon returning to the cave to enlighten the others, he is met with hostility and disbelief.

The allegory highlights the difference between the illusory world of sensory perception and the higher reality accessible through reason and intellectual insight. It underscores Plato's belief that philosophical education is essential for understanding the true nature of reality and achieving enlightenment.

FEBRUARY 5: PLATO - PHILOSOPHER-KINGS SHOULD RULE

I N "THE REPUBLIC," PLATO argues that the ideal society should be governed by philosopher-kings. He believed that those who truly understand the Forms, especially the Form of the Good, are best equipped to rule justly and wisely. According to Plato, philosophers possess the knowledge and virtue necessary to create a harmonious and just society.

Plato's ideal ruler is someone who has undergone rigorous education and has a deep understanding of justice, truth, and the common good. Unlike rulers who seek power for personal gain, philosopher-kings would govern selflessly, guided by their knowledge of the higher truths.

This idea reflects Plato's belief in the importance of wisdom and ethical leadership. He envisioned a society where rulers are chosen based on their intellectual and moral qualities, ensuring that governance is based on reason and justice rather than ambition and greed.

FEBRUARY 6: DIOGENES - ASCETICISM AND SELF-SUFFICIENCY

D IOGENES OF SINOPE, A prominent figure in the Cynic movement, advocated for a life of asceticism and self-sufficiency. He believed that happiness and freedom come from living simply and rejecting material excess. Diogenes famously lived in a large ceramic jar (often mistakenly called a barrel) and owned very few possessions, demonstrating his commitment to minimalism.

Diogenes' lifestyle was a direct critique of the prevailing social norms and materialistic values of his time. He sought to show that true contentment comes from independence and self-discipline rather than wealth and luxury. His asceticism was not just about rejecting material goods but also about cultivating inner strength and self-control.

By living in accordance with nature and focusing on essential needs, Diogenes believed individuals could achieve greater clarity and freedom. His teachings emphasized the importance of self-sufficiency and the rejection of societal expectations.

February 7: Diogenes - Criticism of Social Conventions

D IOGENES WAS KNOWN FOR his sharp criticism of
social conventions and norms. He believed that many
societal practices were irrational and hypocritical, and he
sought to expose their absurdity through provocative acts
and statements. Diogenes often challenged the values and
behaviors of his contemporaries, urging them to reconsider
their priorities and live more authentically.

One famous example is Diogenes' encounter with Alexander the Great. When Alexander offered to grant him any
wish, Diogenes simply replied, "Stand out of my sunlight."
This response highlighted Diogenes' disdain for power and
wealth and his commitment to living a simple, natural life.

Diogenes' criticism extended to various aspects of society,
including politics, religion, and social customs. His goal was
to encourage people to think critically about their beliefs
and practices and to live in accordance with reason and
nature rather than blindly following tradition.

February 8: Diogenes - Embrace of Cynicism

D IOGENES IS OFTEN REGARDED as the archetypal Cynic, embracing a philosophy that values virtue over wealth, power, and fame. Cynicism, in its original sense, advocates for a life in accordance with nature and reason, free from the artificial constraints of society. Diogenes' commitment to Cynicism was reflected in his disdain for materialism and his focus on living a virtuous, self-sufficient life.

One striking example of Diogenes' Cynicism is his habit of carrying a lantern in daylight, claiming to be searching for an honest man. This act was intended to critique the moral corruption he saw around him and to emphasize the rarity of true virtue.

Diogenes' embrace of Cynicism was a call to reject superficial values and to live a life guided by reason and virtue. His teachings encouraged individuals to find contentment in self-sufficiency and to prioritize their moral integrity over societal approval.

FEBRUARY 9: ARISTOTLE - THE GOLDEN MEAN

A RISTOTLE, ONE OF THE greatest philosophers of ancient Greece, introduced the concept of the Golden Mean, which advocates for moderation in all things. According to Aristotle, virtue lies in finding the balance between excess and deficiency. For instance, courage is the mean between recklessness and cowardice. This principle of moderation applies to all aspects of life, encouraging a balanced and harmonious approach to living.

Aristotle illustrated this concept with practical examples. For instance, generosity lies between wastefulness and stinginess, while honesty lies between deceit and bluntness. By identifying the extremes and finding the mean, individuals can cultivate virtuous habits and make balanced decisions.

The Golden Mean reflects Aristotle's broader ethical framework, which emphasizes the importance of practical wisdom and the cultivation of good character. It suggests that achieving virtue requires thoughtful deliberation and the ability to navigate complex moral landscapes.

FEBRUARY 10: ARISTOTLE - EMPIRICISM: KNOWLEDGE THROUGH OBSERVATION

ARISTOTLE CHAMPIONED EMPIRICISM, THE idea that knowledge comes from sensory experience and observation. Unlike his teacher Plato, who emphasized abstract reasoning and the world of Forms, Aristotle believed that true understanding arises from studying the natural world. He conducted extensive empirical research, observing and categorizing plants, animals, and various natural phenomena.

Aristotle's approach laid the groundwork for the scientific method. He believed that by systematically collecting and analyzing data, we can uncover the principles that govern the natural world. His emphasis on observation and experience marked a significant departure from purely theoretical speculation.

One example of Aristotle's empirical work is his classification of living organisms. By carefully studying their physical characteristics and behaviors, he developed a comprehensive system of taxonomy that influenced biological sciences for centuries. His work demonstrates the power of empirical observation in advancing human knowledge.

February 11: Aristotle - Teleology: Purpose in Nature

A RISTOTLE INTRODUCED THE CONCEPT of teleology, which posits that everything in nature has a purpose or end goal (telos). According to Aristotle, understanding an object's purpose is key to understanding its nature. For instance, the purpose of an acorn is to become an oak tree, and the purpose of human life is to achieve eudaimonia, or flourishing.

Aristotle's teleological approach extends to all aspects of life and nature. He believed that natural processes are goal-directed and that each entity's development follows a specific trajectory towards fulfilling its purpose. This perspective shaped his studies in biology, ethics, and metaphysics.

In his ethical writings, Aristotle argued that humans achieve their highest potential by cultivating virtues and fulfilling their rational capacities. By understanding and striving towards our natural purposes, we can lead more meaningful and fulfilling lives. This teleological view underscores Aristotle's belief in the inherent order and purposefulness of the natural world.

FEBRUARY 12: ZHUANGZI - RELATIVITY OF PERCEPTION

Z HUANGZI, AN INFLUENTIAL CHINESE philosopher, emphasized the relativity of perception in his writings. He illustrated this with his famous butterfly dream: Zhuangzi dreamt he was a butterfly, and upon waking, he couldn't determine if he was a man dreaming he was a butterfly or a butterfly dreaming he was a man. This story underscores his belief that our perceptions and experiences are subjective and fluid, challenging the notion of a fixed reality.

Zhuangzi's idea of perception relativity teaches that our understanding of the world is shaped by our perspectives, which can vary greatly from person to person. This concept encourages an open-minded approach to life, where we acknowledge the limitations of our viewpoints and remain open to other interpretations. By embracing this philosophical stance, we can cultivate greater empathy and understanding in our interactions with others.

Through various parables and anecdotes, Zhuangzi illustrated how different creatures perceive the world differently based on their nature. For example, a fish's understanding of water differs from that of a human's. This highlights the importance of considering different perspectives to gain a more comprehensive understanding of reality. Zhuangzi's philosophy invites us to question our assumptions and appreciate the diverse ways in which life can be experienced.

February 13: Zhuangzi - Spontaneity in Life

Z HUANGZI VALUED SPONTANEITY AND naturalness in life, advocating for living in harmony with the Dao (the Way). He believed that true wisdom comes from acting intuitively and effortlessly, without overthinking or forcing situations. This idea is captured in his concept of "wu wei," or "non-action," which emphasizes aligning one's actions with the natural flow of the world.

To illustrate the importance of spontaneity, Zhuangzi used the example of a skilled butcher who effortlessly carves an ox by following the animal's natural contours. This story demonstrates how mastery and effectiveness arise from acting in accordance with nature, rather than through rigid planning or exertion. By embracing spontaneity, we can navigate life's challenges with ease and grace.

Zhuangzi's emphasis on spontaneity encourages us to let go of excessive control and allow things to unfold naturally. This approach can lead to greater creativity and adaptability, as we respond to situations with a flexible and open mind. By trusting our instincts and embracing the flow of life, we can achieve a sense of harmony and fulfillment.

February 14: Zhuangzi - Uselessness can be an Advantage

Z HUANGZI PRESENTED THE IDEA that what appears useless can actually be advantageous. In one of his parables, he describes a gnarled tree that, due to its twisted and misshapen form, is not suitable for lumber and thus spared from being cut down. This tree's "uselessness" ensures its survival, highlighting the unexpected benefits of non-conformity.

This lesson challenges conventional notions of value and utility, suggesting that there is merit in things often deemed worthless. Zhuangzi's philosophy invites us to reconsider what we dismiss as unimportant and recognize the potential hidden within. By doing so, we can appreciate the unique qualities that may not fit traditional criteria but still hold significant value.

Through this concept, Zhuangzi teaches us to find worth in unexpected places and to value diversity and individuality. Just as the gnarled tree thrives because it does not meet standard expectations, individuals can also find strength and resilience in their uniqueness. This perspective encourages a more inclusive and holistic view of value and purpose in life.

FEBRUARY 15: EPICURUS - SEEK SIMPLE PLEASURES

E PICURUS, AN ANCIENT GREEK philosopher, advocated for seeking simple pleasures as the key to a happy life. He believed that the greatest good is to seek modest, sustainable pleasures and avoid unnecessary desires. For Epicurus, pleasure is the absence of pain, both physical and mental, and can be achieved through simple living, friendship, and intellectual pursuits.

Epicurus taught that the pursuit of simple pleasures leads to tranquility and contentment. He advised his followers to focus on basic needs, such as food, shelter, and companionship, rather than chasing after wealth, power, or fame. This approach to life emphasizes the importance of appreciating the small, everyday joys that bring lasting satisfaction.

To illustrate his philosophy, Epicurus often referred to the pleasure of enjoying a simple meal with friends. This example highlights the profound satisfaction that can be found in modest experiences. By prioritizing simple pleasures, we can cultivate a more balanced and fulfilling life, free from the stress and anxiety associated with excessive desires.

February 16: Epicurus - Avoid Pain

C ENTRAL TO EPICURUS' PHILOSOPHY is the principle of avoiding pain. He believed that minimizing physical and mental suffering is essential for achieving a happy life. According to Epicurus, the prudent management of desires and the cultivation of wisdom help prevent the disturbances that lead to pain. He advocated for moderation and thoughtful decision-making to maintain a state of tranquility.

Epicurus distinguished between necessary and unnecessary desires, advising that fulfilling only those essential for well-being helps avoid pain. For instance, the desire for food is necessary, while the craving for luxury is not. By focusing on necessary desires and avoiding those that lead to excess or harm, we can reduce the potential for suffering.

In his letters and teachings, Epicurus emphasized the importance of mental tranquility, or "ataraxia," which is the absence of anxiety and disturbance. He encouraged practices such as philosophical reflection and the cultivation of friendships to achieve this state. By understanding the sources of pain and taking steps to mitigate them, we can lead a more peaceful and contented life.

February 17: Epicurus - The Universe Consists of Atoms and Void

E PICURUS ADOPTED AND EXPANDED upon the atomistic theory of Democritus, asserting that the universe consists of atoms and void. According to this view, everything in the world is composed of tiny, indivisible particles (atoms) moving through empty space (void). Epicurus used this theory to explain natural phenomena and to argue against the existence of supernatural forces.

Epicurus believed that understanding the atomic nature of the universe helps alleviate the fear of gods and death. By explaining that natural events result from the interactions of atoms, he sought to dispel the notion that deities control our fate. This rational perspective encourages a sense of security and freedom from irrational fears.

One example Epicurus used to illustrate his theory was the random motion of atoms, known as "the swerve," which introduces unpredictability into the universe. This concept supports the idea of free will, suggesting that not everything is predetermined. By comprehending the atomic structure of reality, we can better understand the natural world and our place within it.

FEBRUARY 18: XUNZI - HUMANS ARE INHERENTLY SELFISH

XUNZI, A CHINESE CONFUCIAN philosopher, argued that humans are inherently selfish and driven by desires. Unlike Mencius, who believed in the innate goodness of humans, Xunzi maintained that people are born with a propensity for selfishness and need guidance to cultivate virtue. He asserted that through education and moral training, individuals can overcome their base instincts and achieve ethical behavior.

Xunzi used the analogy of a bent piece of wood to illustrate his point. Just as wood must be steamed and straightened to be useful, human nature requires education and discipline to develop virtue. This view emphasizes the importance of external influences and deliberate effort in shaping moral character.

By recognizing the inherent selfishness in human nature, Xunzi highlighted the need for strong social institutions and educational systems to guide individuals toward ethical behavior. His philosophy underscores the significance of nurturing and cultivating virtue through intentional practices and societal structures.

FEBRUARY 19: XUNZI - EDUCATION AND RITUALS CULTIVATE VIRTUE

F OR XUNZI, EDUCATION AND rituals are essential tools for cultivating virtue and transforming human nature. He believed that through rigorous study and participation in rituals, individuals can develop moral character and social harmony. Education provides the knowledge and skills necessary for ethical conduct, while rituals reinforce proper behavior and social norms.

Xunzi saw rituals as a means of channeling human desires and emotions into constructive actions. For example, mourning rituals help individuals express grief in a socially acceptable manner, fostering a sense of community and shared values. These practices teach discipline and respect, essential qualities for maintaining order and harmony in society.

Xunzi's emphasis on education and rituals reflects his belief in the power of culture and tradition to shape human behavior. By engaging in these practices, individuals internalize moral principles and develop a sense of duty and responsibility. This structured approach to moral development highlights the role of external guidance in achieving personal and societal virtue.

February 20: Xunzi - Strong Institutions and Laws Maintain Order

X UNZI ARGUED THAT STRONG institutions and laws are necessary to maintain order and ensure social stability. He believed that human nature, being inherently selfish, requires external constraints to prevent chaos and conflict. By establishing clear rules and effective governance, societies can promote justice and discourage harmful behavior.

Xunzi compared laws and institutions to dikes that control the flow of water. Just as dikes prevent flooding and direct water to beneficial uses, laws regulate human behavior and promote social harmony. This analogy underscores the importance of a well-structured legal system in managing the complexities of human interactions.

In his writings, Xunzi emphasized the need for wise and capable rulers to enforce laws and uphold justice. He believed that good governance is crucial for fostering a stable and prosperous society. Xunzi's philosophy highlights the interplay between individual behavior and institutional structures, advocating for a balanced approach to achieving order and virtue.

FEBRUARY 21: SENECA - ENDURE HARDSHIP WITH RESILIENCE

S ENECA, A ROMAN STOIC philosopher, emphasized the importance of enduring hardship with resilience. He believed that adversity is an inevitable part of life and that true strength lies in how we respond to it. Seneca taught that by cultivating inner strength and maintaining a calm and rational mindset, we can navigate life's challenges without being overwhelmed by them.

In his work "Letters to Lucilius," Seneca provides practical advice on how to develop resilience. He encourages practicing voluntary discomfort, such as fasting or exposing oneself to the cold, to build mental and physical toughness. This practice helps prepare the mind to remain steadfast in the face of unavoidable suffering.

Seneca's approach to resilience is grounded in the Stoic belief that our reactions to events are within our control, even if the events themselves are not. By focusing on our inner responses and developing a resilient mindset, we can maintain our composure and dignity regardless of external circumstances. This perspective is central to Stoic philosophy and Seneca's teachings.

FEBRUARY 22: SENECA - PRACTICAL WISDOM IN LETTERS

SENECA'S "LETTERS TO LUCILIUS" is a collection of moral epistles that offer practical wisdom on various aspects of life. Through these letters, Seneca addresses topics such as friendship, happiness, and the pursuit of virtue. His advice is grounded in Stoic principles, emphasizing rationality, self-discipline, and ethical living.

One key theme in Seneca's letters is the value of time and the importance of using it wisely. He advises Lucilius to avoid wasting time on trivial pursuits and to focus on meaningful activities that contribute to personal growth and the well-being of others. This emphasis on time management reflects Seneca's broader philosophy of living a purposeful life.

Seneca also discusses the importance of self-reflection and continuous self-improvement. He encourages Lucilius to regularly examine his thoughts and actions, striving to align them with Stoic virtues. By doing so, one can cultivate a more fulfilling and virtuous life. Seneca's letters remain relevant today, offering timeless advice on how to live wisely and ethically.

February 23: Seneca - Living in Accordance with Nature

L IVING IN ACCORDANCE WITH nature is a central tenet of Seneca's Stoic philosophy. For Seneca, this means understanding the natural order of the world and our place within it. He believed that by aligning our lives with nature's principles, we can achieve tranquility and fulfillment. This involves accepting what we cannot change and focusing on what is within our control.

Seneca argued that living in accordance with nature requires us to develop virtues such as wisdom, courage, justice, and temperance. These virtues help us navigate life's challenges and maintain inner peace. By cultivating these qualities, we can live harmoniously with the world and ourselves.

In practical terms, Seneca advised embracing simplicity and avoiding excessive desires. He believed that by reducing our attachment to external goods and focusing on inner virtues, we can achieve a state of contentment. This approach to life emphasizes the importance of self-awareness and mindful living, guiding us towards a more balanced and meaningful existence.

February 24: Epictetus - Focus on What is Within Your Control

E PICTETUS, A PROMINENT STOIC philosopher, taught that we should focus on what is within our control and accept what is not. He believed that our thoughts, actions, and attitudes are within our control, while external events and other people's actions are not. This distinction is fundamental to Epictetus' philosophy and is key to achieving tranquility.

In his work "Enchiridion" (The Handbook), Epictetus advises that by focusing on our own responses and letting go of the desire to control external events, we can maintain inner peace. For example, if someone insults us, we cannot control their behavior, but we can control our reaction to it. By choosing not to be offended, we preserve our peace of mind.

Epictetus' teachings emphasize personal responsibility and self-mastery. He encourages us to develop a mindset of acceptance and to cultivate resilience in the face of life's uncertainties. This focus on internal control helps us navigate challenges with a calm and rational attitude, aligning with Stoic ideals.

FEBRUARY 25: EPICTETUS - TRUE FREEDOM THROUGH MASTERY OF DESIRES

E PICTETUS BELIEVED THAT TRUE freedom comes from mastering our desires and passions. He argued that when we are ruled by our desires, we become enslaved to external circumstances and lose our autonomy. By gaining control over our impulses and focusing on what truly matters, we can achieve inner freedom and tranquility.

In his teachings, Epictetus emphasized the importance of distinguishing between what we need and what we merely want. He encouraged his followers to practice self-discipline and to avoid being swayed by fleeting pleasures or societal pressures. This discipline helps us maintain focus on our higher goals and values.

Epictetus used the analogy of a skilled archer to illustrate his point. Just as an archer focuses on perfecting their aim rather than worrying about hitting the target, we should focus on cultivating our inner virtues rather than seeking external validation. By mastering our desires, we gain the freedom to live according to our true nature and values.

FEBRUARY 26: EPICTETUS - STOIC ENDURANCE OF HARDSHIP

S TOIC ENDURANCE OF HARDSHIP is a core principle in Epictetus' philosophy. He taught that adversity is an inevitable part of life and that enduring it with dignity and resilience is crucial for personal growth. Epictetus believed that hardships are opportunities to practice and strengthen our virtues, such as patience, courage, and wisdom.

In his discourses, Epictetus often compared life to a banquet where we must accept whatever is served. This metaphor highlights the importance of accepting circumstances beyond our control and making the best of them. By viewing challenges as tests of character, we can approach them with a constructive mindset.

Epictetus also emphasized the role of mindset in enduring hardship. He advised maintaining a perspective that sees difficulties as temporary and surmountable. By focusing on our inner strength and remaining committed to our principles, we can navigate life's challenges with stoic resilience, maintaining our integrity and inner peace.

M ARCUS AURELIUS, A ROMAN emperor and Stoic philosopher, echoed the teachings of Epictetus by emphasizing the importance of controlling what we can and accepting what we cannot. In his "Meditations," Marcus Aurelius reflects on the transient nature of life and the need to focus on our actions and attitudes rather than external events.

Marcus Aurelius believed that by directing our efforts towards self-improvement and maintaining a rational mindset, we can achieve tranquility. He encouraged practicing mindfulness and self-discipline to remain focused on what truly matters. This approach helps us maintain inner stability amidst external chaos.

In his writings, Marcus Aurelius often reminded himself to remain calm and composed in the face of adversity. By focusing on his own conduct and perspective, he was able to navigate the complexities of ruling an empire while adhering to Stoic principles. His reflections offer timeless advice on how to lead a life of purpose and resilience.

FEBRUARY 28: MARCUS AURELIUS - ACCEPTANCE OF IMPERMANENCE

M ARCUS AURELIUS EMPHASIZED THE acceptance of impermanence as a fundamental aspect of Stoic philosophy. He believed that understanding and accepting the transient nature of life helps us appreciate the present moment and let go of attachments. In his "Meditations," Marcus Aurelius frequently contemplated the impermanence of all things, from personal experiences to the vast expanse of time.

He used the analogy of nature's cycles, such as the changing seasons, to illustrate the inevitability of change. By recognizing that everything has a beginning and an end, we can cultivate a sense of detachment and equanimity. This acceptance allows us to face loss and change with grace and resilience.

Marcus Aurelius encouraged reflecting on the fleeting nature of life to foster gratitude and mindfulness. By appreciating the present and understanding that all things are temporary, we can live more fully and authentically. His reflections remind us of the importance of embracing the impermanence of existence.

February 29: Marcus Aurelius - Fulfill Your Duty Without Complaint

M ARCUS AURELIUS BELIEVED IN fulfilling one's duty without complaint as a central tenet of Stoic philosophy. He emphasized that each person has a role to play in the larger order of the universe, and it is our responsibility to perform our duties to the best of our abilities. In his "Meditations," he frequently reminded himself to approach his responsibilities with diligence and without resentment.

He argued that complaining about our duties only adds unnecessary suffering and distracts us from the task at hand. By accepting our roles and responsibilities, we can focus our energy on productive actions rather than futile resistance. This attitude fosters a sense of purpose and commitment.

Marcus Aurelius' reflections on duty also highlight the importance of maintaining integrity and ethical conduct. He believed that fulfilling our duties with a positive attitude not only benefits ourselves but also contributes to the greater good. His philosophy encourages us to approach our responsibilities with a sense of honor and dedication.

MARCH 1: Nāgārjuna - Middle Way: Avoidance of Extremes in Philosophy

Nāgārjuna, an influential Buddhist philosopher, founded the Madhyamaka school of Mahayana Buddhism. One of his core teachings is the Middle Way, which advocates for the avoidance of extremes in philosophical and practical life. Nāgārjuna argued that clinging to absolute views, whether eternalism or nihilism, leads to misunderstanding and suffering. Instead, he promoted a balanced perspective that transcends these dualities.

Nāgārjuna illustrated the Middle Way by critiquing the inherent existence of things. He emphasized that phenomena arise dependently, meaning they do not exist independently or inherently. This approach encourages a nuanced understanding of reality, avoiding the extremes of asserting or denying existence. By adopting this middle path, one can navigate life with greater wisdom and compassion.

The Middle Way also applies to ethical conduct, where Nāgārjuna advised against extremes of indulgence and asceticism. He believed that a balanced lifestyle fosters mental clarity and spiritual growth. This principle of moderation is central to his teachings, guiding practitioners towards a harmonious and enlightened way of life.

March 2: Nāgārjuna - Emptiness: Concept that Phenomena Lack Intrinsic Nature

Nāgārjuna's doctrine of emptiness (śūnyatā) is a foundational concept in his philosophy. He asserted that all phenomena lack intrinsic nature and exist only through dependent origination. This means that things do not possess an independent, unchanging essence; their existence is contingent upon causes and conditions. Emptiness is not nihilism but a way to understand the interdependent nature of reality.

To illustrate emptiness, Nāgārjuna used the example of a chariot. He explained that a chariot is not an independent entity but a collection of parts assembled in a specific way. Without its parts and their arrangement, the chariot does not exist. Similarly, all phenomena are composites without inherent existence, highlighting the interconnectedness of everything.

Understanding emptiness helps dissolve attachments and aversions, as it reveals the impermanent and interdependent nature of reality. This insight can lead to liberation from suffering, as it fosters a deeper awareness of the fluidity and interrelation of all things. Nāgārjuna's teachings on emptiness challenge us to rethink our assumptions and perceptions.

March 3: Nāgārjuna - Two Truths: Conventional and Ultimate Truth

N ĀGĀRJUNA INTRODUCED THE CONCEPT of two truths: conventional truth and ultimate truth. Conventional truth refers to the everyday reality we experience, characterized by ordinary perceptions and social agreements. Ultimate truth, on the other hand, pertains to the deeper, emptiness-based understanding that all phenomena lack inherent existence. Both truths are essential for comprehending the full nature of reality.

Nāgārjuna used the analogy of a snake and a rope to explain the two truths. Mistaking a rope for a snake represents conventional truth, where our perceptions can be misleading. Recognizing the rope as it truly is symbolizes ultimate truth, where deeper insight dispels illusions. Understanding both truths allows for a more comprehensive grasp of reality.

The interplay between conventional and ultimate truth is crucial for spiritual practice. Nāgārjuna emphasized that while ultimate truth provides profound insight into the nature of existence, conventional truth is necessary for practical living and ethical conduct. Balancing these perspectives enables a harmonious and enlightened approach to life, integrating wisdom and compassion.

March 4: Plotinus - The One

P LOTINUS, A MAJOR FIGURE in Neoplatonism, introduced the concept of "The One," the ultimate principle
of reality. The One is the source of all existence, transcending all forms and qualities. It is absolute unity and simplicity, beyond comprehension and description. Plotinus believed that The One is the foundation from which everything
emanates, sustaining the cosmos and all beings within it.

Plotinus used the analogy of the sun and its rays to explain
The One's relationship with the world. Just as the sun remains unchanged while its rays extend outward, The One
remains transcendent while its emanations give rise to the
multiplicity of existence. This perspective emphasizes the
interconnectedness of all things and their dependence on a
single, ultimate source.

Understanding The One invites contemplation of the unity underlying the diversity of the world. Plotinus taught
that through philosophical inquiry and inner purification,
individuals can experience mystical union with The One.
This process involves transcending the material world and
realizing the divine nature within, leading to spiritual fulfillment and enlightenment.

MARCH 5: PLOTINUS - EMANATION

E MANATION IS A CENTRAL concept in Plotinus' philosophy, describing the process by which all things originate from The One. According to Plotinus, The One, being perfect and self-sufficient, overflows and generates the Intellect (Nous), which in turn emanates the Soul (Psyche), and finally the material world. Each level of emanation reflects a decrease in purity and unity, moving further from The One.

Plotinus used the metaphor of light radiating from a source to illustrate emanation. The closer to the source, the brighter and purer the light; as it extends outward, it becomes dimmer and more diffuse. This hierarchy reflects the gradations of reality, from the highest, most unified principle to the diverse and fragmented material world.

Emanation emphasizes the dynamic and interconnected nature of existence. Plotinus believed that by understanding this process, individuals could trace their origins back to The One and aspire to return to their divine source. This philosophical framework offers a path for spiritual ascent, emphasizing contemplation and inner transformation.

March 6: Plotinus - Mystical Union

M YSTICAL UNION WITH THE One is the ultimate goal in Plotinus' philosophy. He believed that through deep contemplation and inner purification, the soul can transcend the material world and achieve direct, intuitive knowledge of The One. This union is characterized by a profound sense of unity and dissolution of the self, merging with the absolute source of all existence.

Plotinus described mystical union as an ecstatic experience, where the individual transcends the limitations of the physical body and intellect. In this state, the soul encounters The One in a pure, unmediated form, experiencing absolute simplicity and unity. This union is not a permanent state but a fleeting moment of profound insight and spiritual fulfillment.

Plotinus emphasized that the path to mystical union involves rigorous philosophical training, ethical living, and ascetic practices. By refining the soul and detaching from material desires, individuals can prepare themselves for this transformative experience. Plotinus' teachings on mystical union highlight the possibility of attaining ultimate reality and divine communion through inner development.

March 7: Augustine of Hippo - Original Sin

A UGUSTINE OF HIPPO, A foundational figure in Christian philosophy, introduced the doctrine of original sin. He believed that humanity inherited sin from Adam and Eve's disobedience in the Garden of Eden. According to Augustine, original sin corrupts human nature, making people inherently inclined towards wrongdoing and necessitating divine grace for salvation.

Augustine used the analogy of a hereditary disease to explain original sin. Just as a disease can be passed from parent to child, sin is transmitted from generation to generation, affecting all of humanity. This concept underscores the idea that human beings are born with a flawed nature that they cannot overcome through their own efforts.

Original sin plays a crucial role in Augustine's theology, emphasizing the need for redemption through Christ. He argued that only through divine grace can individuals be cleansed of sin and restored to a state of righteousness. This doctrine highlights the importance of faith and divine intervention in achieving spiritual salvation.

I N HIS SEMINAL WORK "The City of God," Augustine of Hippo contrasts two realms: the City of God and the City of Man. The City of God represents the community of believers who live according to divine will, seeking eternal peace and salvation. The City of Man, on the other hand, embodies the secular world driven by self-interest and earthly desires.

Augustine used the fall of Rome to illustrate the transient nature of the City of Man. He argued that earthly kingdoms are temporary and prone to corruption, while the City of God is eternal and unshakeable. This distinction emphasizes the Christian perspective that true fulfillment and security lie in the divine realm, not in worldly achievements.

The City of God vs. City of Man dichotomy highlights the tension between spiritual aspirations and earthly concerns. Augustine believed that while Christians must live in the world, their ultimate allegiance should be to God's kingdom. This framework guides believers to prioritize spiritual values and seek a deeper connection with the divine.

March 9: Augustine of Hippo - Faith and Reason

A UGUSTINE OF HIPPO INTEGRATED faith and reason in his philosophical and theological writings. He believed that faith and reason are complementary, with faith providing the foundation for understanding and reason offering tools to deepen and articulate that faith. For Augustine, true knowledge begins with belief in God and is further illuminated through rational inquiry.

Augustine used the metaphor of the "light of faith" to describe how divine illumination guides human understanding. He argued that faith provides the initial insight necessary to comprehend higher truths, while reason helps explore and explain these truths in greater detail. This approach affirms that both faith and reason are essential for a complete and coherent worldview.

In his work "Confessions," Augustine demonstrated how his intellectual journey was deeply intertwined with his spiritual quest. He used philosophical reasoning to address theological questions and personal struggles, showing that faith and reason together lead to a richer, more profound understanding of reality. Augustine's integration of faith and reason has profoundly influenced Christian thought and philosophy.

March 10: Proclus - Neoplatonism: Hierarchical Universe

P ROCLUS, A PROMINENT NEOPLATONIST philosopher, elaborated on the hierarchical structure of the universe. He believed that reality is organized in a series of levels, with The One at the highest point, followed by the Intellect (Nous), the Soul (Psyche), and finally the material world. Each level emanates from the one above it, reflecting a gradation of purity and unity.

Proclus used the metaphor of a chain of light to describe this hierarchy. The closer to the source, the brighter and purer the light; as it extends outward, it becomes dimmer and more fragmented. This hierarchical model explains the diversity and complexity of the world while maintaining a unified underlying principle.

The hierarchical universe in Proclus' philosophy emphasizes the interconnectedness of all things. He believed that by understanding this structure, individuals could aspire to ascend through the levels of reality, ultimately seeking union with The One. This framework provides a path for spiritual growth and enlightenment, grounded in the principles of Neoplatonism.

MARCH 11: PROCLUS - THE ONE: SOURCE OF ALL EXISTENCE

F OR PROCLUS, THE ONE is the ultimate source of all existence, transcending all categories and distinctions. The One is absolute unity and simplicity, beyond comprehension and description. Proclus believed that everything in the universe emanates from The One, which sustains and unifies all beings and phenomena.

Proclus used the analogy of the sun to illustrate The One's relationship with the universe. Just as the sun remains unchanged while its light illuminates all things, The One remains transcendent while its emanations give rise to the multiplicity of existence. This analogy highlights the infinite and ineffable nature of The One.

Understanding The One is central to Proclus' Neoplatonism. He taught that through philosophical contemplation and inner purification, individuals could attain a deeper connection with The One. This process involves transcending the material world and realizing the divine source within, leading to spiritual fulfillment and mystical union.

MARCH 12: PROCLUS - THEURGY: RITUAL PRACTICES TO INVOKE THE DIVINE

T HEURGY, OR DIVINE WORK, is a key aspect of Proclus' philosophy. He believed that through ritual practices, individuals could invoke the presence and power of the divine, facilitating a closer connection with higher realities. Theurgy involves the use of symbols, invocations, and sacred rituals to align the soul with the divine order.

Proclus saw theurgy as a way to bridge the gap between the material and spiritual worlds. He argued that these rituals help purify the soul and elevate it towards the divine, enabling a direct experience of the higher realms. Theurgy complements philosophical contemplation, providing a practical means of spiritual ascent.

Proclus emphasized that theurgy requires proper understanding and reverence. It is not merely a set of mechanical actions but a profound spiritual practice aimed at achieving union with the divine. By engaging in theurgy, individuals can experience the presence of the gods and gain insight into the deeper mysteries of existence, aligning their lives with the divine order.

MARCH 13: BOETHIUS - CONSOLATION OF PHILOSOPHY

B OETHIUS, A ROMAN PHILOSOPHER, wrote "The Consolation of Philosophy" while imprisoned, facing execution. This influential work is a dialogue between Boethius and Lady Philosophy, who offers him comfort and wisdom. The text addresses issues of fortune, happiness, and the nature of good and evil. Boethius reflects on the fleeting nature of earthly possessions and the importance of seeking inner peace.

In "The Consolation of Philosophy," Boethius contemplates the role of fortune in human life. He describes how fortune is unpredictable and often unjust, bringing both joy and suffering. Lady Philosophy reminds him that true happiness cannot depend on such unstable and external factors. Instead, she guides him towards finding contentment within himself, through virtue and wisdom.

Boethius' work emphasizes the enduring value of philosophical inquiry, especially in times of personal crisis. By engaging with philosophical ideas, he finds solace and a deeper understanding of his situation. "The Consolation of Philosophy" continues to resonate with readers for its timeless exploration of the human condition and the search for meaning.

March 14: Boethius - Eternal vs. Temporal

B OETHIUS EXPLORED THE DISTINCTION between the eternal and the temporal in "The Consolation of Philosophy." He argued that true reality is eternal and unchanging, unlike the temporal world, which is marked by constant change and impermanence. For Boethius, the eternal is associated with the divine and ultimate truth, while the temporal is linked to the material world and human experience.

He used the metaphor of a wheel of fortune to illustrate the transient nature of temporal success and failure. As the wheel turns, one's position can change rapidly, symbolizing the unpredictability of worldly life. In contrast, the eternal remains constant and unaffected by the passage of time. Boethius believed that understanding this distinction helps us focus on what truly matters.

Boethius' insights encourage a philosophical perspective on life, where the pursuit of eternal truths and virtues takes precedence over temporary gains and losses. By recognizing the limits of the temporal world, we can aspire to connect with the eternal aspects of existence, finding deeper meaning and purpose.

March 15: Boethius - True Happiness Comes from Within

BOETHIUS TAUGHT THAT TRUE happiness comes from within, independent of external circumstances. In "The Consolation of Philosophy," he argued that relying on external factors such as wealth, power, and fame for happiness is misguided. These external goods are unstable and can be taken away, leading to inevitable disappointment and suffering.

Lady Philosophy advises Boethius to seek happiness in the cultivation of virtue and wisdom. She explains that the highest good is found within the soul, in living a life aligned with reason and moral integrity. This inner source of happiness is resilient and enduring, unlike the fleeting pleasures of the external world.

Boethius' message is a call to focus on personal development and the pursuit of inner peace. By nurturing our inner virtues and understanding the true nature of happiness, we can attain a sense of fulfillment that remains steadfast, regardless of external changes and challenges.

March 16: Empedocles - Four Elements: Earth, Air, Fire, Water

E MPEDOCLES, A PRE-SOCRATIC PHILOSOPHER, proposed that all matter is composed of four fundamental
elements: earth, air, fire, and water. These elements combine
and separate through the forces of love and strife, which
govern the processes of creation and destruction in the
natural world. Empedocles' theory was an early attempt to
explain the diversity and change observed in nature.

He used the analogy of a painter mixing colors to describe
how the elements combine in different proportions to create
various forms of matter. For example, rocks are primarily
composed of earth, while clouds are made mostly of air and
water. This framework provided a basis for understanding
the composition and transformation of substances.

Empedocles' theory of the four elements influenced later
philosophical and scientific thought, including the development of classical Greek and medieval alchemy. His ideas
represent an important step in the quest to understand the
fundamental building blocks of the natural world and the
dynamic processes that shape it.

March 17: Empedocles - Love and Strife: Forces Driving Change

E MPEDOCLES INTRODUCED THE CONCEPTS of love and strife as the two fundamental forces driving change in the universe. Love (philia) brings elements together, creating harmony and unity, while strife (neikos) separates them, leading to discord and fragmentation. These opposing forces are in constant interplay, shaping the cycles of creation and destruction.

He used the metaphor of a cosmic cycle to illustrate how love and strife operate. During periods dominated by love, the elements are united into harmonious forms. Conversely, during times of strife, the elements are pulled apart, leading to chaos and dissolution. This cyclical process explains the continual transformation of the natural world.

Empedocles' theory highlights the balance between opposing forces as essential to the dynamic nature of reality. By understanding the roles of love and strife, we gain insight into the mechanisms of change and the underlying unity of the cosmos. His ideas underscore the importance of balance and harmony in the natural order.

March 18: Empedocles - Theory of Reincarnation

E MPEDOCLES ALSO PROPOSED A theory of reincarnation, believing that souls undergo a cycle of rebirths in
different forms. He taught that souls are immortal and move
through various bodies as part of their journey towards
purification and enlightenment. This cycle continues until
the soul attains a state of divine purity and returns to the
realm of the gods.

He used the metaphor of exile to describe the soul's journey,
likening it to a divine being cast out of its heavenly home
and wandering through various earthly forms. This process
is seen as both a punishment for past wrongs and an opportunity for spiritual growth and redemption.

Empedocles' belief in reincarnation reflects his broader
cosmological and ethical views, emphasizing the interconnectedness of all life and the possibility of spiritual transformation. His ideas influenced later philosophical and religious traditions, contributing to the development of concepts of karma and rebirth in both Western and Eastern
thought.

March 19: Chandrakirti - Madhyamaka: Middle Way Philosophy in Buddhism

C HANDRAKIRTI, A SIGNIFICANT FIGURE in Mahayana Buddhism, is known for his contributions to Madhyamaka, or Middle Way philosophy. This school of thought, founded by Nāgārjuna, advocates for a path that avoids extremes and embraces a balanced approach to understanding reality. Chandrakirti elaborated on this by emphasizing the importance of seeing beyond dualistic thinking and recognizing the interdependent nature of all phenomena.

He used the example of dependent origination to illustrate the Middle Way. According to this principle, everything arises in dependence on conditions and lacks inherent existence. This perspective helps to avoid the extremes of eternalism (believing in inherent existence) and nihilism (denying existence altogether), promoting a more nuanced understanding of reality.

Chandrakirti's teachings on the Middle Way encourage practitioners to cultivate wisdom and compassion by recognizing the interconnectedness of all things. This approach not only guides philosophical inquiry but also informs ethical conduct and spiritual practice, leading to a more balanced and enlightened way of living.

MARCH 20: CHANDRAKIRTI - EMPTINESS: ALL PHENOMENA ARE EMPTY OF INHERENT EXISTENCE

C HANDRAKIRTI EMPHASIZED THE CONCEPT of emptiness (śūnyatā) in his philosophical writings. He taught that all phenomena are empty of inherent existence, meaning they do not possess an independent, unchanging essence. Instead, everything exists in dependence on causes and conditions, reflecting a dynamic and interconnected reality.

He used the example of a chariot to explain emptiness. A chariot is not an independent entity but a collection of parts assembled in a specific way. Without its parts and their arrangement, the chariot does not exist. Similarly, all phenomena are composites without inherent existence, highlighting their dependent nature.

Understanding emptiness helps dissolve attachments and aversions, as it reveals the impermanent and interdependent nature of reality. This insight can lead to liberation from suffering, as it fosters a deeper awareness of the fluidity and interrelation of all things. Chandrakirti's teachings on emptiness challenge us to rethink our assumptions and perceptions.

March 21: Chandrakirti - Dependent Origination: Interdependence of All Things

C HANDRAKIRTI'S EXPLORATION OF DEPENDENT origination is central to his Madhyamaka philosophy. He taught that all phenomena arise in dependence on a web of interrelated causes and conditions. This principle explains the interconnectedness of all things, showing that nothing exists in isolation or possesses an independent essence.

He illustrated dependent origination using the example of a sprout growing from a seed. The sprout's existence depends on the seed, soil, water, sunlight, and numerous other factors. Without these conditions, the sprout would not arise. This analogy underscores the idea that everything is part of a vast, interdependent network.

Chandrakirti's emphasis on dependent origination encourages a holistic view of reality, where the relationships between phenomena are acknowledged and valued. This perspective fosters a deeper understanding of the complexity and interdependence of the world, guiding both philosophical inquiry and practical living.

March 22: John Scotus Eriugena - The Division of Nature

J OHN SCOTUS ERIUGENA, A medieval philosopher and theologian, proposed a comprehensive framework in his work "Periphyseon" (The Division of Nature). He divided nature into four categories: the uncreated creating (God), the created creating (the primordial causes), the created uncreating (the physical world), and the uncreated uncreating (God as the ultimate return). This schema aims to explain the relationship between the divine and the material world.

Eriugena used the metaphor of a circle to describe this process. The divine emanates the primordial causes, which generate the physical world. Ultimately, all creation returns to its divine source, completing the circle. This cyclical model reflects the unity and interconnectedness of all aspects of reality.

The Division of Nature offers a vision of the universe where the material and spiritual realms are intimately connected. Eriugena's framework emphasizes the continuity between creation and the divine, suggesting that understanding the natural world can lead to insights into the divine nature.

MARCH 23: JOHN SCOTUS ERIUGENA - THEOLOGY AS A SCIENCE

J OHN SCOTUS ERIUGENA VIEWED theology as a science, integrating reason and faith in his philosophical approach. He believed that rational inquiry and philosophical analysis are essential tools for understanding theological truths. Eriugena's synthesis of reason and faith reflects his confidence in the harmony between divine revelation and human intellect.

He used the example of light to illustrate his point. Just as light illuminates objects, reason illuminates theological truths, making them comprehensible to the human mind. Eriugena argued that true knowledge comes from the interplay of reason and faith, where each complements and enhances the other.

Eriugena's perspective on theology as a science highlights the importance of intellectual rigor and critical thinking in religious study. His approach encourages a deep and nuanced exploration of faith, where philosophical reasoning is employed to deepen and articulate spiritual insights, leading to a more profound understanding of the divine.

March 24: John Scotus Eriugena - Universal Salvation

E RIUGENA'S DOCTRINE OF UNIVERSAL salvation is one of his most distinctive and controversial ideas. He believed that all creation would ultimately be reconciled with God, achieving a state of unity and harmony. This belief is based on his understanding of the divine nature as all-encompassing and inherently good, ensuring that no part of creation is permanently excluded from salvation.

He used the metaphor of a river returning to the sea to illustrate this concept. Just as all rivers eventually flow back into the ocean, all souls will ultimately return to their divine source. This process reflects the infinite mercy and love of God, who desires the salvation of all beings.

Eriugena's doctrine of universal salvation challenges traditional notions of eternal damnation, offering a more inclusive and optimistic vision of the divine plan. His ideas emphasize the ultimate unity and redemption of all creation, suggesting that the journey towards God is universal and all-encompassing.

MARCH 25: AL-FARABI - VIRTUOUS CITY

AL-FARABI, A PROMINENT ISLAMIC philosopher, introduced the concept of the virtuous city in his work "The Virtuous City." He envisioned an ideal society governed by reason and virtue, where leaders are philosophers who possess wisdom and moral integrity. Al-Farabi's virtuous city is modeled after Plato's philosopher-kings, emphasizing the role of enlightened leadership in achieving social harmony.

He used the analogy of the human body to describe the virtuous city. Just as the body functions harmoniously when each part performs its proper role, the city thrives when each citizen fulfills their duties according to their abilities and virtues. This model highlights the importance of cooperation and justice in creating a well-ordered society.

Al-Farabi's concept of the virtuous city underscores the connection between individual virtue and collective well-being. By cultivating wisdom and moral character in both leaders and citizens, a society can achieve true happiness and prosperity, reflecting the harmony between reason and ethical conduct.

MARCH 26: AL-FARABI - PHILOSOPHY AND RELIGION

A L-FARABI BELIEVED IN THE complementary relationship between philosophy and religion. He argued that both disciplines seek the same ultimate truth, though they approach it through different means. Philosophy uses reason and intellectual inquiry, while religion employs symbolic and allegorical language to convey profound truths to a broader audience.

He used the example of light to illustrate this relationship. Philosophy is like the direct light of the sun, offering clear and immediate illumination, while religion is like the moon, reflecting the sun's light in a more accessible form. Both sources of light guide people towards understanding and truth.

Al-Farabi's integration of philosophy and religion emphasizes the value of both rational and spiritual approaches to knowledge. His perspective encourages a harmonious coexistence of intellectual inquiry and religious faith, promoting a more comprehensive and inclusive understanding of truth.

March 27: Al-Farabi - Blending Greek Philosophy with Islamic Thought

A L-FARABI IS RENOWNED FOR blending Greek philosophy, particularly that of Plato and Aristotle, with Islamic thought. He believed that the insights of Greek philosophers could enrich Islamic philosophy, providing a robust framework for understanding the natural world, ethics, and metaphysics. Al-Farabi's synthesis aimed to harmonize reason and revelation.

He used the example of Aristotle's logic to enhance Islamic theological and philosophical discussions. By applying Aristotelian principles of logic and reasoning, Al-Farabi sought to clarify and strengthen Islamic doctrines, making them more coherent and defensible. This approach highlights the universality of philosophical inquiry.

Al-Farabi's blending of Greek philosophy with Islamic thought paved the way for future Islamic philosophers, such as Avicenna and Averroes. His work demonstrates the potential for cross-cultural intellectual exchange, enriching both traditions and contributing to the development of a global philosophical heritage.

March 28: Avicenna (Ibn Sina) - Essence and Existence

A VICENNA, ALSO KNOWN AS Ibn Sina, was a Persian polymath who made significant contributions to philosophy and medicine. One of his key philosophical ideas is the distinction between essence and existence. Avicenna argued that essence (what a thing is) and existence (that a thing is) are fundamentally different. For him, essence refers to the defining characteristics of a thing, while existence refers to the actualization of that essence in reality.

He used the example of a mythical creature, like a unicorn, to explain this concept. The essence of a unicorn (a horse with a horn) can be understood, but its existence is another matter—unicorns do not exist in reality. This distinction laid the groundwork for later philosophical discussions on the nature of being and influenced both Islamic and Western thought.

Avicenna's distinction between essence and existence highlights the complexity of understanding what things are and whether they exist. It challenges us to think deeply about the nature of reality and our assumptions about what constitutes existence. His work set the stage for future philosophical inquiries into the nature of being and existence.

MARCH 29: AVICENNA (IBN SINA) - FLYING MAN THOUGHT EXPERIMENT

AVICENNA'S "FLYING MAN" THOUGHT experiment is one of his most famous contributions to philosophy. In this thought experiment, he asks us to imagine a person created fully formed in mid-air, with no sensory experiences or contact with the outside world. Despite lacking sensory input, Avicenna argues that this person would still be aware of their own existence. This thought experiment is used to demonstrate the self-awareness and self-evident nature of the soul.

This experiment emphasizes the idea that self-awareness does not depend on physical sensation or external experiences. It suggests that the soul's existence is known innately and directly, independent of the body. Avicenna's thought experiment was a significant development in the philosophy of mind and influenced later thinkers like Descartes.

The Flying Man thought experiment highlights the importance of introspection and self-awareness in understanding the nature of the self. It challenges us to consider the fundamental aspects of our consciousness and the nature of our existence beyond physical experiences. This thought experiment remains a powerful tool for exploring philosophical questions about the mind and self-awareness.

March 30: Avicenna (Ibn Sina) - Empirical Observation in Medicine

A VICENNA MADE SUBSTANTIAL CONTRIBUTIONS to medicine, emphasizing the importance of empirical observation and experimentation. His seminal work, "The Canon of Medicine," was a comprehensive medical encyclopedia that integrated knowledge from various cultures and emphasized the importance of clinical observation and systematic experimentation in diagnosing and treating illnesses.

He used detailed case studies and empirical evidence to develop his medical theories. For example, Avicenna carefully documented the symptoms and progression of diseases, and he advocated for testing treatments through controlled observation. His approach to medicine was innovative for its time and laid the foundation for modern clinical practice.

Avicenna's emphasis on empirical observation underscores the importance of evidence-based practice in medicine. His work demonstrates how careful observation and systematic investigation can lead to significant advancements in medical knowledge and practice. Avicenna's contributions to medicine continue to influence the field today, highlighting the enduring value of empirical research.

MARCH 31: ANSELM OF CANTERBURY - ONTOLOGICAL ARGUMENT

A NSELM OF CANTERBURY, A medieval philosopher and theologian, is best known for formulating the ontological argument for the existence of God. This argument is based on the concept that God, being defined as the greatest conceivable being, must exist in reality because existence is a necessary attribute of the greatest conceivable being. Anselm argued that the very concept of God implies His existence.

He used the analogy of a painter conceiving a painting to illustrate his argument. Just as a painting exists in the painter's mind before it is realized on canvas, the concept of God exists in the mind, but unlike the painting, God must exist in reality because the greatest conceivable being cannot lack existence. This argument seeks to demonstrate that denying God's existence is logically contradictory.

Anselm's ontological argument has been both influential and controversial, inspiring numerous debates and further developments in philosophical theology. It challenges us to consider the relationship between concepts and existence, and the nature of logical reasoning in understanding profound metaphysical questions.

April 1: Anselm of Canterbury - Faith Seeking Understanding

ANSELM FAMOUSLY DESCRIBED HIS theological approach as "faith seeking understanding." He believed that faith in God is the starting point, and that reason and intellectual inquiry should follow to deepen and articulate that faith. Anselm saw no conflict between faith and reason; instead, he viewed them as complementary, with reason serving to enhance and clarify the insights provided by faith.

He used the metaphor of a person ascending a hill to describe this process. Faith is the initial step, providing the motivation to begin the climb, while reason is the path that helps one reach the summit and gain a clearer, more comprehensive view. This approach emphasizes the dynamic interplay between belief and intellectual exploration.

Anselm's perspective on faith and reason encourages a holistic approach to theology and philosophy, where belief and rational inquiry work together to achieve a deeper understanding of divine truths. His view has influenced many subsequent thinkers and remains a foundational concept in Christian philosophy.

April 2: Anselm of Canterbury - Divine Attributes: Necessary and Perfect

A NSELM'S PHILOSOPHICAL THEOLOGY ALSO explored the nature of divine attributes, emphasizing that God possesses all perfections necessarily and inherently. He argued that attributes such as omnipotence, omniscience, and perfect goodness are essential qualities of God, defining His nature. Anselm maintained that these attributes are not contingent or arbitrary but are integral to the concept of God.

He used the concept of necessary existence to explain these attributes. Just as God's existence is necessary and not contingent, so are His perfections. For example, God's omnipotence means that He has unlimited power by necessity, not by choice. This framework underscores the absolute and perfect nature of the divine being.

Anselm's exploration of divine attributes provides a philosophical basis for understanding the nature of God in terms of perfection and necessity. His ideas have significantly influenced theological and philosophical discussions about the nature of divinity and the logical coherence of attributing specific qualities to the concept of God.

APRIL 3: PETER ABELARD - SIC ET NON (YES AND NO)

P ETER ABELARD, A MEDIEVAL philosopher and theologian, is known for his work "Sic et Non" ("Yes and
No"). In this work, Abelard compiled a list of seemingly
contradictory statements from the Church Fathers on various theological issues. His goal was to demonstrate the
complexity of theological debates and to encourage critical
thinking and dialectical reasoning to resolve apparent contradictions.

He used the method of presenting conflicting authorities
to stimulate debate and analysis. By juxtaposing opposing
viewpoints, Abelard aimed to show that theological inquiry
requires careful interpretation and synthesis of different
perspectives. This approach highlights the importance of
critical examination and reasoned argument in theological
discourse.

"Sic et Non" played a crucial role in the development of
scholasticism, a method of learning that emphasizes dialectical reasoning and systematic analysis. Abelard's work
encouraged scholars to engage deeply with theological texts,
fostering a tradition of rigorous intellectual inquiry that
shaped medieval philosophy and theology.

April 4: Peter Abelard - Ethical Intentions

A BELARD MADE SIGNIFICANT CONTRIBUTIONS to ethics, particularly with his focus on the role of intention in moral evaluation. He argued that the morality of an action depends not solely on its consequences or adherence to rules, but on the intention behind it. For Abelard, an action is morally good if it is done with a good intention, even if the outcome is less than ideal.

He used the example of a person giving alms to illustrate his point. If someone gives to the poor out of genuine compassion, the action is morally praiseworthy. However, if the same action is done for selfish reasons, such as seeking praise, it lacks true moral value. This emphasis on intention highlights the internal aspect of morality.

Abelard's focus on ethical intentions influenced later philosophical and theological discussions on morality. His ideas encourage a deeper examination of the motivations behind actions, contributing to a more nuanced understanding of ethical behavior and the nature of moral responsibility.

April 5: Peter Abelard - Conceptualism

A BELARD IS ALSO KNOWN for his contributions to the philosophy of language and his development of conceptualism. Conceptualism is the view that universals exist not as independent entities but as concepts in the mind. Abelard argued that while universal terms like "humanity" or "redness" do not exist independently, they are useful for categorizing and understanding the world through mental concepts.

He used the example of language to explain conceptualism. Words like "tree" or "dog" refer to categories that exist in our minds, helping us to organize and communicate our experiences. These concepts do not exist outside the mind, but they are essential for understanding and interacting with the world.

Abelard's conceptualism provides a middle ground between realism and nominalism, offering a way to understand the existence of universals through the lens of mental constructs. His ideas have influenced subsequent debates in the philosophy of language and the nature of universals, contributing to the development of medieval and modern thought.

April 6: Averroes (Ibn Rushd) - Double Truth

A VERROES, ALSO KNOWN AS Ibn Rushd, was a medieval Andalusian philosopher who introduced the concept of double truth. This idea posits that religious and philosophical truths can coexist independently, each with its own domain. According to Averroes, religious truths are based on faith and revelation, while philosophical truths are derived from reason and empirical observation.

He used the analogy of two paths leading to the same destination to explain double truth. One path represents faith, guiding believers through religious teachings, while the other path represents reason, guiding philosophers through logical inquiry. Both paths ultimately lead to the same truth, but they operate in different ways.

Averroes' concept of double truth aimed to reconcile conflicts between religion and philosophy, suggesting that both can provide valid and complementary insights into reality. His ideas influenced later medieval thought and contributed to the ongoing dialogue between faith and reason in Western and Islamic philosophy.

April 7: Averroes (Ibn Rushd) - Reinterpreting Aristotle for Islam

A VERROES MADE SIGNIFICANT CONTRIBUTIONS by reinterpreting Aristotle's works within an Islamic context. He sought to harmonize Aristotelian philosophy with Islamic theology, arguing that both could coexist and complement each other. Averroes believed that Aristotle's emphasis on reason and empirical observation could enhance the understanding of Islamic teachings.

He used the example of Aristotle's ethics to illustrate this integration. Averroes argued that Aristotle's concept of the golden mean, which advocates for moderation and balance in all things, aligns with Islamic principles of ethical conduct. By reinterpreting Aristotle, Averroes aimed to show that rational philosophy and religious faith could mutually reinforce each other.

Averroes' work in reinterpreting Aristotle for Islam played a crucial role in preserving and transmitting Greek philosophy to the medieval West. His commentaries on Aristotle were later translated into Latin and significantly influenced European scholasticism, bridging the intellectual traditions of the Islamic world and the West.

April 8: Averroes (Ibn Rushd) - Critique of Al-Ghazali

A VERROES IS WELL-KNOWN FOR his critique of Al-Ghazali, an influential Islamic theologian who argued against the use of philosophy in understanding religious truths. In his work "The Incoherence of the Philosophers," Al-Ghazali criticized philosophers for straying from Islamic teachings. In response, Averroes wrote "The Incoherence of the Incoherence," defending the use of philosophy and reason in religion.

He used logical arguments to counter Al-Ghazali's claims, asserting that philosophy and religion are not mutually exclusive but can support and enrich each other. Averroes argued that the Quran encourages the use of reason and intellectual inquiry, and that understanding the natural world through philosophy can enhance one's appreciation of divine creation.

Averroes' critique of Al-Ghazali emphasized the importance of reason and philosophical inquiry in religious life. His defense of philosophy as a legitimate and valuable tool for understanding faith helped shape the intellectual landscape of the Islamic world and contributed to the broader discourse on the relationship between faith and reason.

APRIL 9: MAIMONIDES - NEGATIVE THEOLOGY

M AIMONIDES, A MEDIEVAL JEWISH philosopher and theologian, is renowned for his development of negative theology. This approach to theology asserts that we can only describe God by what He is not, rather than by what He is. Maimonides believed that God's essence is beyond human comprehension, and any positive attributes we assign to Him are inadequate and potentially misleading.

He used the analogy of light to illustrate this concept. Just as we can describe light by stating what it is not (not darkness, not cold), we can speak of God by negating imperfections. This method helps avoid anthropomorphism and ensures that our understanding of God remains transcendent and mysterious.

Maimonides' negative theology highlights the limits of human language and intellect in describing the divine. By focusing on what God is not, we maintain a sense of reverence and humility, acknowledging the infinite and incomprehensible nature of the divine. This approach has influenced both Jewish and Christian mystical traditions.

April 10: Maimonides - Guide for the Perplexed

M AIMONIDES' "GUIDE FOR THE Perplexed" is a seminal work that addresses the challenges faced by those who struggle to reconcile religious faith with philosophical inquiry. In this book, Maimonides provides philosophical interpretations of Jewish scriptures, aiming to demonstrate that religious teachings and rational philosophy can coexist harmoniously.

He used the example of biblical anthropomorphisms, such as descriptions of God having a physical form, to illustrate his approach. Maimonides argued that such descriptions are metaphorical, intended to make complex theological concepts accessible to human understanding. By interpreting these metaphors philosophically, he aimed to resolve apparent contradictions between scripture and reason.

The "Guide for the Perplexed" has had a profound impact on Jewish thought and has influenced Christian and Islamic philosophy as well. Maimonides' work encourages a thoughtful and critical approach to religious texts, promoting a deeper understanding of faith through the lens of reason.

April 11: Maimonides - Ethics through Moderation and Wisdom

MAIMONIDES EMPHASIZED THE IMPORTANCE of moderation and wisdom in ethical conduct. He believed that virtuous living involves finding a balance between extremes, aligning with the Aristotelian concept of the golden mean. For Maimonides, wisdom is the guiding principle that helps individuals navigate moral dilemmas and make balanced decisions.

He used the example of generosity to illustrate this idea. True generosity, according to Maimonides, lies between the extremes of miserliness and prodigality. A wise person gives appropriately, without depriving themselves or overextending their resources. This balanced approach ensures that ethical actions are sustainable and beneficial.

Maimonides' emphasis on moderation and wisdom in ethics underscores the importance of thoughtful deliberation and self-awareness in moral decision-making. His teachings encourage individuals to cultivate virtues through reasoned reflection and practical wisdom, fostering a harmonious and fulfilling life.

April 12: Thomas Aquinas - Natural Law

T HOMAS AQUINAS, A MEDIEVAL philosopher and theologian, is known for his integration of Aristotelian
philosophy with Christian theology. One of his significant
contributions is the theory of natural law. Aquinas argued
that natural law is a set of moral principles inherent in
human nature, accessible through reason. These principles
guide human behavior and reflect the divine order of creation.

Aquinas used the example of the inclination to preserve
life to illustrate natural law. He believed that humans, by
nature, seek to protect and sustain their lives, which aligns
with the moral principle of valuing and preserving life. This
natural inclination is a manifestation of natural law, guiding
individuals towards morally right actions.

Aquinas' theory of natural law influenced later thinkers,
including Enlightenment philosophers like John Locke. It
provides a foundation for understanding morality based on
human nature and reason, bridging the gap between philosophy and theology. His work underscores the compatibility
of reason and faith in discerning ethical principles.

April 13: Thomas Aquinas - Five Ways to Prove God's Existence

T HOMAS AQUINAS FORMULATED FIVE arguments for the existence of God, known as the Five Ways, in his work "Summa Theologica." These arguments are rooted in observation and logical reasoning, aiming to demonstrate God's existence through empirical evidence and rational thought. The Five Ways include the Argument from Motion, the Argument from Causation, the Argument from Contingency, the Argument from Degree, and the Argument from Final Cause or Teleology.

Aquinas' Argument from Motion posits that everything in motion must be moved by something else, ultimately leading to an unmoved mover, which he identifies as God. This argument reflects Aristotelian influence, emphasizing the need for a prime mover to explain motion in the universe.

Aquinas' Five Ways have been debated and critiqued by later philosophers, such as David Hume and Immanuel Kant. Nonetheless, they remain foundational in the philosophy of religion, providing a systematic approach to demonstrating God's existence through reason and empirical observation. Aquinas' integration of Aristotelian philosophy with Christian theology exemplifies his intellectual rigor and enduring influence.

April 14: Thomas Aquinas - Faith and Reason Complement Each Other

T HOMAS AQUINAS IS RENOWNED for his belief that faith and reason are complementary, not contradictory. He argued that reason and empirical evidence can lead to certain truths about the natural world and God, while faith provides deeper insights into divine mysteries that transcend human understanding. Aquinas believed that both faith and reason originate from God, and therefore, they cannot truly conflict.

Aquinas used the example of understanding God's nature to illustrate this harmony. Through reason, one can infer the existence of God and some of His attributes, such as omnipotence and goodness. Faith, however, reveals deeper truths, such as the Trinity and the Incarnation, which surpass the limits of human reason. This dual approach enriches the understanding of divine truth.

Aquinas' synthesis of faith and reason influenced later Christian thought and the development of scholasticism. His work laid the groundwork for subsequent theologians and philosophers, demonstrating that rigorous intellectual inquiry and deep religious faith can coexist and enrich each other.

April 15: Meister Eckhart - Mystical Union with God

M EISTER ECKHART, A GERMAN mystic and theologian, is known for his teachings on the mystical union with God. He believed that the soul could achieve direct, experiential knowledge of God through a process of inner purification and detachment from worldly concerns. Eckhart's mysticism emphasizes the immediate presence of God within the soul, transcending conventional religious practices and doctrines.

Eckhart used the metaphor of a spark to describe the soul's union with God. He taught that within each soul lies a divine spark, which can be awakened and united with God through contemplation and spiritual discipline. This union brings about a profound sense of peace and enlightenment, where the soul experiences God directly.

Eckhart's mystical teachings influenced later Christian mystics, such as Teresa of Ávila and John of the Cross. His emphasis on the inner experience of God offers a deeply personal approach to spirituality, encouraging believers to seek a direct and transformative relationship with the divine.

April 16: Meister Eckhart - The Ground of Being

M EISTER ECKHART INTRODUCED THE concept of the "Ground of Being" to describe the fundamental essence of God and all existence. He believed that God is the ultimate reality, the source from which all things emerge and to which they return. This Ground of Being is beyond all attributes and descriptions, representing the absolute and infinite nature of God.

Eckhart used the analogy of a tree and its roots to explain this concept. Just as the roots are the unseen source that nourishes and sustains the tree, the Ground of Being is the underlying reality that supports all existence. Understanding this deep connection helps individuals realize their unity with God and all creation.

Eckhart's idea of the Ground of Being has resonated with various philosophical and theological traditions, including existentialism and process theology. His teachings invite a contemplative exploration of the fundamental nature of existence and our relationship with the divine, emphasizing the profound interconnectedness of all life.

April 17: Meister Eckhart - Detachment and Inner Peace

DETACHMENT IS A CENTRAL theme in Meister Eckhart's spiritual teachings. He believed that achieving inner peace and union with God requires detaching oneself from worldly attachments and desires. This detachment is not about renouncing the world but about freeing oneself from the ego's grip and cultivating a state of inner stillness and openness to God.

Eckhart used the example of a clean, empty vessel to illustrate detachment. Just as a vessel must be empty to be filled, the soul must be free from attachments to be receptive to God's presence. This state of inner emptiness allows for a deeper connection with the divine, fostering true peace and contentment.

Eckhart's emphasis on detachment and inner peace has influenced various spiritual traditions, including contemplative Christianity and Zen Buddhism. His teachings encourage individuals to cultivate an inner life that transcends external circumstances, focusing on the transformative power of spiritual practice and inner awareness.

April 18: William of Ockham - Ockham's Razor

WILLIAM OF OCKHAM, A medieval philosopher and theologian, is best known for Ockham's Razor, a principle of simplicity and parsimony in reasoning. Ockham's Razor states that when presented with competing hypotheses, one should select the one that makes the fewest assumptions. This principle encourages simplicity and clarity in scientific and philosophical explanations.

Ockham used the example of explaining celestial motions. Instead of positing numerous complex mechanisms, he argued that one should adopt the simplest explanation that fits the observed data. This approach minimizes unnecessary complexity and focuses on the most straightforward, plausible account of phenomena.

Ockham's Razor has had a lasting impact on scientific methodology and philosophy, promoting a preference for simplicity and elegance in theoretical frameworks. It remains a valuable heuristic tool for evaluating and refining hypotheses in various fields of inquiry.

April 19: William of Ockham - Nominalism

W ILLIAM OF OCKHAM IS also known for his advocacy of nominalism, the philosophical view that universals do not have independent existence but are merely names or labels for sets of individual objects. According to Ockham, only particular entities exist, and universals are simply mental constructs used for convenience in language and thought.

He used the example of "redness" to illustrate nominalism. Ockham argued that redness does not exist as a universal entity but is a concept we use to describe all red objects. Each red object is an individual entity, and "redness" is a term that groups these entities based on a shared characteristic.

Ockham's nominalism challenged the prevailing realist views of his time and influenced later philosophical debates about the nature of universals and language. His emphasis on the particular and the individual contributed to the development of modern empirical and scientific approaches to understanding the world.

April 20: William of Ockham - Divine Omnipotence

W ILLIAM OF OCKHAM'S THEOLOGICAL views emphasized the absolute omnipotence of God. He argued that God's will is not bound by any external constraints or logical necessities, highlighting God's ultimate freedom and power. Ockham believed that God can do anything that is logically possible, underscoring the importance of divine will in shaping the order of creation.

He used the example of moral laws to illustrate divine omnipotence. Ockham argued that moral laws are contingent on God's will and could have been different if God had so chosen. This perspective emphasizes the idea that God's power is not limited by human conceptions of morality or rationality.

Ockham's views on divine omnipotence sparked significant theological debates and influenced later discussions on the nature of God's power and freedom. His emphasis on the absolute sovereignty of God's will highlights the profound and often paradoxical relationship between divine omnipotence and human understanding.

APRIL 21: ERASMUS - PRAISE OF FOLLY: CRITIQUE OF CHURCH AND SOCIETY

E RASMUS OF ROTTERDAM, A Renaissance humanist, is best known for his satirical work "Praise of Folly." In this book, Folly personified delivers a witty and incisive critique of contemporary church practices and societal norms. Erasmus used humor and irony to highlight the corruption, hypocrisy, and absurdities within the church and broader society, calling for reform and a return to genuine piety.

He used the example of church officials accumulating wealth and power while neglecting their spiritual duties to illustrate his critique. By portraying these officials as foolish and self-serving, Erasmus emphasized the need for humility, simplicity, and devotion in religious life.

"Praise of Folly" became a seminal work of the Renaissance, influencing the Protestant Reformation and the broader movement for religious and social reform. Erasmus' use of satire and humanist ideals helped shape the intellectual landscape of his time, advocating for a more authentic and humane approach to faith and society.

April 22: Erasmus - Humanism: Emphasis on Human Values

E RASMUS WAS A LEADING figure in the Renaissance humanist movement, which emphasized the value and dignity of the individual, the importance of education, and the study of classical texts. Humanism sought to revive the intellectual and cultural achievements of ancient Greece and Rome, promoting a balanced and holistic approach to knowledge and personal development.

He used the example of classical education to illustrate the principles of humanism. Erasmus advocated for the study of Greek and Latin literature, philosophy, and history as a means of cultivating virtuous and well-rounded individuals. This education aimed to develop critical thinking, moral integrity, and a deep appreciation for human creativity and achievement.

Erasmus' humanist ideals influenced the development of modern education and the humanities, promoting a vision of learning that integrates intellectual, moral, and aesthetic dimensions. His work underscores the enduring relevance of humanist principles in fostering a more enlightened and compassionate society.

APRIL 23: ERASMUS - EDUCATION: ADVOCATING FOR REFORM

E RASMUS WAS A PASSIONATE advocate for educational reform, believing that a well-rounded and morally grounded education was essential for personal and societal development. He argued for a curriculum that emphasized not only intellectual skills but also ethical and spiritual growth. Erasmus believed that education should cultivate wisdom, virtue, and a love for learning.

He used the example of his book "On the Education of a Christian Prince" to illustrate his vision for education. In this work, Erasmus outlined the qualities and virtues that a ruler should possess, emphasizing the importance of a broad and humane education in developing just and enlightened leaders.

Erasmus' advocacy for educational reform had a lasting impact on the development of modern educational systems. His emphasis on critical thinking, moral education, and the study of classical texts helped shape the liberal arts tradition and continues to inspire educators and students today.

APRIL 24: NICCOLÒ MACHIAVELLI - THE ENDS JUSTIFY THE MEANS

NICCOLÒ MACHIAVELLI, A RENAISSANCE political philosopher, is best known for his work "The Prince," where he famously argues that the ends justify the means. Machiavelli believed that rulers must be pragmatic and willing to use any means necessary, including deception and cruelty, to achieve and maintain power. This perspective challenges traditional moral and ethical considerations in political leadership.

He used the example of Cesare Borgia, a ruthless and cunning leader, to illustrate his point. Machiavelli admired Borgia's ability to consolidate power and achieve his goals, despite his ruthless tactics. This example highlights the importance of effective leadership and the willingness to make difficult decisions in the pursuit of political stability.

Machiavelli's ideas have been both criticized and praised for their realistic and unflinching view of political power. His work remains influential in political theory, offering a stark and sometimes controversial perspective on the complexities of leadership and statecraft.

APRIL 25: NICCOLÒ MACHIAVELLI - POLITICAL REALISM

M ACHIAVELLI IS OFTEN REGARDED as the father of political realism, a theory that emphasizes the importance of power, pragmatism, and practicality in political decision-making. He argued that political leaders should focus on the realities of power rather than idealistic notions of morality. For Machiavelli, the primary goal of a ruler is to ensure the stability and security of the state.

He used the example of military strategy to illustrate political realism. Machiavelli believed that a successful ruler must be adept in the art of war and willing to use force when necessary. This approach emphasizes the need for strategic thinking and adaptability in the face of changing political circumstances.

Machiavelli's political realism has influenced a wide range of political thinkers, from Thomas Hobbes to contemporary political scientists. His work provides a framework for understanding the dynamics of power and the practical considerations that underpin effective governance.

April 26: Niccolò Machiavelli - Virtù and Fortuna

MACHIAVELLI INTRODUCED THE CONCEPTS of virtù and fortuna in his political writings. Virtù refers to a ruler's ability to shape their destiny through strength, skill, and cunning. Fortuna, on the other hand, represents the unpredictable forces of luck and chance that can impact political outcomes. Machiavelli argued that successful leaders must possess virtù to navigate and control fortuna.

He used the metaphor of a river to explain this relationship. Just as a skilled engineer can build dams and channels to control the flow of a river, a wise ruler uses virtù to manage the forces of fortuna. This analogy highlights the importance of proactive and adaptive leadership in achieving political success.

Machiavelli's concepts of virtù and fortuna offer a nuanced understanding of the interplay between human agency and external circumstances in political life. His insights continue to be relevant in discussions of leadership, strategy, and the role of chance in shaping historical events.

April 27: Nicolaus Copernicus - Heliocentrism

NICOLAUS COPERNICUS, A RENAISSANCE astronomer, revolutionized our understanding of the cosmos with his heliocentric theory. He proposed that the Sun, not the Earth, is at the center of the solar system. This was a radical departure from the geocentric model, which placed the Earth at the center of the universe, a view that had dominated Western thought for centuries.

Copernicus' heliocentric model was detailed in his seminal work, "On the Revolutions of the Celestial Spheres." He used extensive mathematical calculations and astronomical observations to support his theory. This model explained the apparent retrograde motion of planets and provided a more straightforward explanation for celestial phenomena, which were overly complicated in the geocentric framework.

The heliocentric theory laid the groundwork for future astronomers like Galileo and Kepler, who further refined and validated Copernicus' ideas. His work marked the beginning of the Scientific Revolution, challenging the established worldview and paving the way for modern astronomy and science.

April 28: Nicolaus Copernicus - Mathematical Astronomy

C OPERNICUS' CONTRIBUTIONS TO ASTRONOMY were not limited to his heliocentric theory; he also emphasized the importance of mathematical precision in astronomical observations. He believed that mathematical calculations could provide more accurate and predictive models of celestial movements. His use of mathematics to describe planetary orbits was a significant advancement over previous, more qualitative approaches.

In "On the Revolutions of the Celestial Spheres," Copernicus presented detailed tables of planetary positions, calculated based on his heliocentric model. These tables allowed for more precise predictions of celestial events, such as eclipses and planetary alignments. His rigorous application of mathematics to astronomy influenced later scientists, including Johannes Kepler, who used Copernican principles to develop his own laws of planetary motion.

Copernicus' focus on mathematical astronomy exemplifies the shift towards empirical and quantitative methods in science. His work demonstrated that mathematical models could provide a deeper understanding of the natural world, a principle that remains fundamental to scientific inquiry today.

April 29: Nicolaus Copernicus - Challenges to Geocentric Model

C OPERNICUS FACED SIGNIFICANT CHALLENGES in promoting his heliocentric model, primarily due to the deeply entrenched geocentric model supported by both scientific and religious authorities of his time. The geocentric model, championed by Ptolemy and endorsed by the Catholic Church, positioned Earth at the center of the universe, a view that seemed intuitively correct based on everyday observations.

To challenge this model, Copernicus meticulously gathered observational data and developed mathematical arguments to support the heliocentric theory. He addressed the apparent contradictions of the geocentric model, such as the complex and convoluted paths of planets, by showing that these could be more simply explained by a Sun-centered system. Despite the elegance and accuracy of his model, Copernicus' ideas were initially met with skepticism and resistance.

The eventual acceptance of Copernicus' heliocentric theory was facilitated by the work of subsequent scientists like Galileo and Kepler, who provided further evidence and refined the model. Copernicus' challenge to the geocentric view exemplifies the transformative power of questioning established beliefs and pursuing scientific truth.

April 30: Michel de Montaigne - Essays: Personal Reflections on Human Nature

M ICHEL DE MONTAIGNE, A French Renaissance philosopher, is best known for his "Essays," a collection of personal reflections on a wide range of topics, including human nature, society, and philosophy. Montaigne's essays are characterized by their introspective and conversational tone, offering a candid exploration of his thoughts and experiences.

Montaigne used the essay format to examine everyday life and philosophical questions, blending anecdotes, historical references, and personal reflections. His essays cover diverse subjects such as friendship, education, and mortality, providing insights into the complexities of human behavior and thought. Montaigne's willingness to share his doubts, uncertainties, and contradictions made his work relatable and engaging.

Montaigne's essays influenced later writers and philosophers, including Francis Bacon and Ralph Waldo Emerson. His approach to writing, characterized by self-examination and a skeptical attitude towards accepted norms, paved the way for modern essayists and the development of personal and philosophical literature.

May 1: Michel de Montaigne - Skepticism: Doubt as a Tool for Understanding

M ONTAIGNE IS ALSO RENOWNED for his skepticism, which he employed as a tool for understanding and navigating the complexities of life. He believed that doubt and questioning are essential for intellectual growth and self-awareness. Montaigne's skepticism was not a form of cynicism but a method of critically examining beliefs and assumptions.

He used the example of cultural relativism to illustrate his skeptical approach. Montaigne observed that customs and beliefs vary widely across cultures, leading him to question the universality of any single perspective. This recognition of diversity in human practices and thought fostered a more open-minded and tolerant view of the world.

Montaigne's skepticism has influenced the development of modern critical thinking and philosophy. His emphasis on doubt and inquiry encourages a reflective and inquisitive mindset, promoting a deeper understanding of oneself and the world.

May 2: Michel de Montaigne - Self-Knowledge: Importance of Introspection

S ELF-KNOWLEDGE AND INTROSPECTION ARE central themes in Montaigne's essays. He believed that understanding oneself is the foundation for understanding others and navigating life's challenges. Montaigne's introspective approach involved a candid examination of his own thoughts, emotions, and experiences, offering insights into the human condition.

He used personal anecdotes and reflections to explore broader philosophical questions. For example, in his essay "On Experience," Montaigne discusses his own health and aging process to delve into the nature of human existence and the limits of knowledge. This introspective method allows readers to relate their own experiences to Montaigne's observations, fostering a deeper connection to his philosophical insights.

Montaigne's emphasis on self-knowledge has had a lasting impact on psychology, literature, and philosophy. His approach encourages individuals to engage in honest self-reflection and to embrace their complexities and contradictions, leading to greater self-awareness and personal growth.

MAY 3: GIORDANO BRUNO - INFINITE UNIVERSE

G IORDANO BRUNO, AN ITALIAN philosopher and cos-
mologist, is best known for his revolutionary ideas
about the universe. He proposed that the universe is infinite
and contains countless worlds similar to our own. Bruno's
views challenged the geocentric and finite universe models
dominant at the time, extending the Copernican heliocentric theory to its logical conclusion.

Bruno used the analogy of stars as suns to support his theory.
He argued that if the Sun is just one star among many, then
other stars could also have planets orbiting them, potentially harboring life. This idea of an infinite universe populated
by numerous worlds was radical and ahead of its time, laying
the groundwork for modern cosmology.

Bruno's bold ideas on the infinite universe were met with
fierce opposition from the Catholic Church, ultimately
leading to his execution for heresy. Despite his tragic fate,
Bruno's vision of an infinite cosmos has profoundly influenced scientific and philosophical thought, anticipating
later developments in astronomy and the understanding of
the universe.

MAY 4: GIORDANO BRUNO - PANTHEISM

G IORDANO BRUNO ALSO ADVANCED the concept of pantheism, the belief that God is identical with the universe and everything in it. According to Bruno, God is not a separate, transcendent entity but is immanent in all aspects of the natural world. This view contrasts with traditional theistic notions of a distinct, personal deity.

Bruno used the metaphor of a single substance to explain pantheism. He argued that just as different shapes can be formed from the same clay, all things in the universe are manifestations of a single divine substance. This perspective emphasizes the unity and interconnectedness of all existence, where the divine is present in every part of the cosmos.

Bruno's pantheistic views challenged conventional religious doctrines and contributed to his condemnation by the Church. However, his ideas have influenced later thinkers, such as Baruch Spinoza, and have continued to inspire discussions on the nature of divinity and the relationship between God and the universe.

MAY 5: GIORDANO BRUNO - COPERNICAN THEORY

G IORDANO BRUNO WAS A fervent supporter and proponent of the Copernican theory, which posited that
the Earth revolves around the Sun. Bruno's endorsement of
heliocentrism went beyond Copernicus' original ideas, as
he proposed an even more expansive and dynamic cosmos.
He argued that the Copernican model was a step towards
understanding the true nature of the universe.

He used the example of the apparent motion of stars to
support the Copernican theory. Bruno suggested that the
observed movements of stars could be better explained by
an infinite universe with countless suns, rather than a finite,
Earth-centered cosmos. His advocacy for heliocentrism was
part of his broader vision of a boundless and ever-changing
universe.

Bruno's support for the Copernican theory placed him at
odds with the religious and scientific authorities of his
time, leading to his persecution. Despite this, his bold and
imaginative ideas contributed to the advancement of astronomical knowledge and the eventual acceptance of the
heliocentric model.

MAY 6: FRANCIS BACON - EMPIRICISM

F RANCIS BACON, AN ENGLISH philosopher and statesman, is often credited with developing the empirical
method, which emphasizes observation and experimentation as the basis for knowledge. Bacon believed that true
understanding of the natural world comes from direct observation and systematic experimentation, rather than from
abstract reasoning or reliance on authority.

He used the example of studying plants to illustrate empiricism. Bacon argued that by carefully observing and exper-
imenting with plants, one could discover their properties
and how they grow, leading to practical applications in agriculture and medicine. This hands-on approach to learning
about the natural world exemplifies the empirical method.

Bacon's emphasis on empiricism laid the foundation for
the modern scientific method, influencing later scientists
like Galileo and Newton. His work underscores the importance of evidence-based inquiry and the role of observation
in developing scientific knowledge, principles that remain
central to scientific practice today.

MAY 7: FRANCIS BACON - SCIENTIFIC METHOD

F RANCIS BACON IS RENOWNED for formalizing the scientific method, a systematic approach to investigation that involves observation, experimentation, and the formulation of hypotheses. Bacon believed that the scientific method was essential for overcoming the limitations of human perception and biases, enabling a more accurate understanding of the natural world.

He used the analogy of a courtroom to describe the scientific method. Just as a judge evaluates evidence to reach a verdict, scientists must gather empirical data and test hypotheses through controlled experiments. This process ensures that conclusions are based on objective evidence rather than preconceived notions or speculative reasoning.

Bacon's development of the scientific method marked a significant shift in the pursuit of knowledge, emphasizing the importance of empirical evidence and systematic inquiry. His ideas laid the groundwork for modern science, promoting a rigorous and methodical approach to understanding the natural world.

May 8: Francis Bacon - Four Idols of the Mind

F RANCIS BACON IDENTIFIED FOUR "idols of the mind" that obstruct clear thinking and hinder scientific progress. These idols are systematic errors and biases that distort human perception and reasoning. Bacon categorized them as Idols of the Tribe, Idols of the Cave, Idols of the Marketplace, and Idols of the Theatre.

He used the example of the Idols of the Tribe to illustrate cognitive biases inherent in human nature. These idols represent the tendency to see patterns where none exist and to generalize from limited experience. This bias can lead to faulty conclusions and hinder objective analysis.

The Idols of the Cave are individual biases shaped by personal experiences and preferences. The Idols of the Marketplace arise from the misuse of language, leading to misunderstandings. The Idols of the Theatre are philosophical dogmas and erroneous belief systems that cloud judgment. By identifying and overcoming these idols, Bacon aimed to promote a more rational and empirical approach to knowledge.

MAY 9: GALILEO GALILEI - HELIOCENTRISM

G ALILEO GALILEI, AN ITALIAN astronomer and physicist, is best known for his support and refinement of the Copernican heliocentric theory. Through his use of the telescope, Galileo provided compelling evidence that challenged the geocentric model. His observations of the moons of Jupiter, the phases of Venus, and the detailed features of the Moon supported the idea that not all celestial bodies revolve around the Earth.

He used the example of the phases of Venus to support heliocentrism. Galileo observed that Venus exhibited a full set of phases similar to the Moon, which could only be explained if Venus orbited the Sun. This observation provided strong evidence against the geocentric model, which could not account for the phases of Venus.

Galileo's advocacy for heliocentrism and his use of empirical evidence revolutionized astronomy and laid the groundwork for modern physics. His work exemplifies the transformative power of scientific observation and critical thinking in challenging established beliefs and advancing human knowledge.

May 10: Galileo Galilei - Empirical Evidence Over Speculation

G ALILEO GALILEI EMPHASIZED THE importance of empirical evidence over speculative reasoning in scientific inquiry. He believed that direct observation and experimentation were essential for understanding the natural world, a view that challenged the reliance on philosophical speculation and dogma that dominated much of medieval science.

He used the example of his experiments with falling bodies to illustrate this approach. Contrary to Aristotle's belief that heavier objects fall faster than lighter ones, Galileo's experiments from the Leaning Tower of Pisa demonstrated that all objects fall at the same rate regardless of their mass. This empirical evidence contradicted long-held theoretical assumptions and advanced the understanding of motion.

Galileo's commitment to empirical evidence transformed scientific methodology, reinforcing the value of observation and experimentation. His work paved the way for the development of classical mechanics and the broader acceptance of the scientific method as the foundation for acquiring knowledge.

May 11: Galileo Galilei - Conflict Between Science and Religion

G ALILEO GALILEI'S SUPPORT FOR the heliocentric model brought him into conflict with the Catholic Church, highlighting the tension between scientific discovery and religious doctrine. Galileo's findings, which supported Copernicus' heliocentrism, contradicted the Church's geocentric interpretation of Scripture, leading to accusations of heresy.

He used his observations of celestial bodies to challenge the Church's teachings. Despite the evidence he provided, such as the moons orbiting Jupiter and the phases of Venus, the Church maintained its geocentric stance. Galileo's defense of heliocentrism eventually led to his trial by the Inquisition and house arrest.

Galileo's conflict with the Church underscores the challenges faced by scientific innovation in the face of established religious and ideological beliefs. His struggle exemplifies the ongoing dialogue between science and religion, highlighting the importance of intellectual freedom and the pursuit of truth in advancing human understanding.

MAY 12: THOMAS HOBBES - SOCIAL CONTRACT

T HOMAS HOBBES, AN ENGLISH philosopher, is best known for his work on political philosophy, particularly his theory of the social contract. Hobbes believed that in the state of nature, human life would be "solitary, poor, nasty, brutish, and short," driven by constant fear and competition. To escape this chaotic state, individuals agree to form a social contract, relinquishing certain freedoms in exchange for security and order provided by a centralized authority.

Hobbes used the metaphor of the "Leviathan," a powerful, sovereign ruler, to illustrate this concept. In his seminal work "Leviathan," he argued that only a strong, centralized authority could maintain peace and prevent the anarchy of the state of nature. This authority derives its legitimacy from the consent of the governed, who agree to abide by common rules for mutual benefit.

Hobbes' ideas on the social contract influenced later political philosophers such as John Locke and Jean-Jacques Rousseau. His work laid the foundation for modern political theory, highlighting the necessity of governance and the balance between individual liberty and collective security.

MAY 13: THOMAS HOBBES - LEVIATHAN: CENTRALIZED AUTHORITY

IN "LEVIATHAN," THOMAS HOBBES elaborated on the need for a centralized authority to maintain social order and prevent conflict. He argued that in the absence of such authority, society would descend into chaos, as individuals pursued their self-interests without regard for others. The Leviathan, or sovereign ruler, embodies the collective will of the people and enforces laws to ensure stability and security.

Hobbes used the example of a commonwealth to illustrate the structure and function of the Leviathan. He described it as an artificial person, representing the unity of its subjects, who collectively empower the sovereign to act on their behalf. This centralized authority has absolute power to legislate, adjudicate, and enforce laws, ensuring that societal order is maintained.

Hobbes' advocacy for a strong, centralized authority contrasts with the more liberal views of philosophers like John Locke, who emphasized limited government and individual rights. Despite this, Hobbes' work remains a cornerstone of political philosophy, offering a pragmatic perspective on the necessity of governance and the role of authority in maintaining social order.

May 14: Thomas Hobbes - Human Nature: Selfish and Competitive

T HOMAS HOBBES HAD A rather pessimistic view of human nature, describing it as inherently selfish and competitive. He believed that individuals are driven by a desire for self-preservation and personal gain, which leads to constant competition and conflict in the absence of societal constraints. This view of human nature underpins his arguments for the social contract and the necessity of a strong, centralized authority.

Hobbes used the example of the state of nature to illustrate his view. In this hypothetical condition, individuals have no common power to keep them in check, leading to a "war of all against all." This state of perpetual conflict and insecurity can only be resolved by individuals agreeing to form a society governed by a sovereign authority that can enforce peace and cooperation.

Hobbes' depiction of human nature influenced later philosophers and political theorists, including those who challenged his views. His portrayal of humanity as fundamentally self-interested continues to provoke debate and discussion, highlighting the complexities of human behavior and the foundations of political order.

May 15: René Descartes - Cogito, Ergo Sum

René Descartes, a French philosopher and mathematician, is famous for his statement "Cogito, ergo sum" ("I think, therefore I am"). This declaration forms the foundation of his philosophy, emphasizing the certainty of one's own existence as the starting point for all knowledge. Descartes sought to establish a secure basis for science and philosophy by doubting all that could be doubted, arriving at the indubitable truth of his own existence as a thinking being.

Descartes used the method of doubt to strip away all uncertain beliefs, leaving only what could be known with absolute certainty. He argued that while sensory experiences and physical reality could be deceptive, the act of thinking itself was undeniable. The very process of doubting one's existence confirms the presence of a thinking entity, hence "I think, therefore I am."

Descartes' cogito has had a profound impact on modern philosophy, shaping the development of epistemology and the philosophy of mind. His emphasis on doubt and rational inquiry laid the groundwork for the Enlightenment and influenced subsequent thinkers such as John Locke and Immanuel Kant.

May 16: René Descartes - Method of Doubt

R ENÉ DESCARTES DEVELOPED THE method of doubt as a systematic process to establish a firm foundation for knowledge. By questioning the certainty of all beliefs, Descartes aimed to identify those that could withstand rigorous scrutiny. This method involves doubting everything that can be doubted, including sensory perceptions, until one reaches beliefs that are absolutely indubitable.

Descartes used the example of dreaming to illustrate his method. He noted that dreams can be so vivid and realistic that they are indistinguishable from waking experiences. This led him to question the reliability of sensory perceptions and seek a more certain basis for knowledge. Through this process, he arrived at the cogito—"I think, therefore I am"—as a foundational truth that cannot be doubted.

Descartes' method of doubt has influenced various fields, including philosophy, science, and psychology. It encourages a rigorous and critical approach to inquiry, emphasizing the importance of questioning assumptions and seeking certainty in knowledge. His method continues to be a fundamental aspect of philosophical methodology.

MAY 17: RENÉ DESCARTES - MIND-BODY DUALISM

RENÉ DESCARTES IS ALSO known for his theory of mind-body dualism, which posits that the mind and body are distinct substances with different properties. According to Descartes, the mind is a non-material, thinking substance, while the body is a material, extended substance. This dualistic view addresses the nature of consciousness and the relationship between mental and physical states.

Descartes used the example of a piece of wax to illustrate his argument. He noted that the sensory properties of the wax (shape, texture, smell) change when it is melted, but the wax itself remains the same substance. This led him to conclude that the essence of the wax is not its sensory properties but its extension in space, accessible through the intellect rather than the senses.

Descartes' mind-body dualism has had a significant impact on the philosophy of mind and the development of psychology. It has influenced debates on the nature of consciousness, the relationship between mental and physical states, and the possibility of life after death. Despite challenges from materialist and monist perspectives, Descartes' dualism remains a foundational concept in the study of the mind.

MAY 18: BLAISE PASCAL - PASCAL'S WAGER

B LAISE PASCAL, A FRENCH mathematician, physicist, and philosopher, is known for his argument known as Pascal's Wager. This pragmatic argument posits that belief in God is a rational bet, even in the absence of conclusive evidence for His existence. Pascal argued that the potential benefits of believing in God (eternal happiness) far outweigh the potential costs (finite earthly sacrifices), making belief a rational choice.

Pascal used the analogy of a wager to explain his argument. He suggested that if God exists and one believes, the reward is infinite (eternal bliss). If God does not exist, the believer loses little or nothing. Conversely, if one does not believe and God exists, the loss is infinite (eternal damnation). Therefore, wagering on belief in God is the safer and more rational bet.

Pascal's Wager has sparked extensive debate and discussion in philosophy and theology. While some criticize it for promoting belief based on self-interest rather than genuine faith, others appreciate its practical approach to addressing existential questions. Pascal's argument continues to influence discussions on faith, reason, and the rationality of religious belief.

May 19: Blaise Pascal - Human Nature: Duality of Greatness and Wretchedness

B LAISE PASCAL HAD A nuanced view of human nature, emphasizing its dual aspects of greatness and
wretchedness. He believed that humans possess both the
capacity for greatness, reflected in their intellect and moral
aspirations, and the potential for wretchedness, evident in
their weaknesses and moral failings. This duality is central
to Pascal's philosophical and theological reflections.

Pascal used the example of human reasoning to illustrate
this duality. He admired the human intellect's ability to
explore and understand the universe, considering it a reflection of humanity's greatness. At the same time, he recognized the limitations and errors of human reasoning,
highlighting the potential for confusion and misjudgment,
which he saw as aspects of human wretchedness.

Pascal's exploration of human nature resonates with existentialist and modern philosophical thought, addressing
the complexities and contradictions inherent in the human
condition. His recognition of both the noble and flawed
aspects of humanity offers a profound and balanced perspective on the human experience, influencing subsequent
philosophical and theological discussions.

May 20: Blaise Pascal - Mysticism: Heart's Reasons Beyond Rational Understanding

B LAISE PASCAL ALSO DELVED into mysticism, asserting that there are truths accessible to the heart that
reason alone cannot grasp. He famously said, "The heart
has its reasons which reason knows nothing of." Pascal believed that religious faith and mystical experiences provide a
deeper understanding of God and existence that transcends
rational analysis.

Pascal used the example of faith to illustrate this idea. He
argued that faith involves an intuitive and emotional connection to God, which goes beyond logical arguments and
evidence. This mystical approach to understanding emphasizes the importance of personal experience and inner conviction in spiritual matters.

Pascal's emphasis on the heart's reasons complements his
rational arguments, such as Pascal's Wager, providing a
holistic view of human understanding that integrates both
reason and emotion. His insights into mysticism have influenced religious thought and highlight the importance of
acknowledging the limits of rationality in comprehending
the full depth of human experience.

May 21: Baruch Spinoza - Pantheism: God and Nature as One

B ARUCH SPINOZA, A DUTCH philosopher, is renowned for his pantheistic view that God and Nature are one and the same. In his magnum opus, "Ethics," Spinoza argued that God is not a transcendent, personal deity but the infinite, eternal substance that constitutes all of reality. Everything that exists is a manifestation of God, and understanding nature is equivalent to understanding God.

Spinoza used the analogy of a wave to explain his pantheism. Just as a wave is a mode of the ocean, individual entities are modes of the single, infinite substance that is God. This perspective emphasizes the unity and interconnectedness of all things, where God is present in everything and everything is a part of God.

Spinoza's pantheism challenged traditional religious views and influenced later philosophical and scientific thought. His ideas resonate with modern ecological and holistic perspectives, highlighting the profound connection between the divine and the natural world. Spinoza's work continues to inspire discussions on the nature of divinity and the relationship between God and the universe.

May 22: Baruch Spinoza - Determinism: Everything Happens Through Necessity

B ARUCH SPINOZA WAS A strong proponent of determinism, the view that all events are determined by necessity and that nothing happens by chance. In "Ethics," he argued that everything in the universe, including human actions and thoughts, follows from the nature of God or Nature with the same necessity as the properties of a triangle follow from its definition.

Spinoza used the example of a stone in motion to illustrate determinism. He argued that if a stone is thrown, its trajectory is determined by the forces acting upon it. Similarly, human actions are determined by internal and external causes, and free will is an illusion. Understanding these causal relationships is key to understanding the natural order.

Spinoza's determinism has influenced various fields, including psychology, neuroscience, and philosophy. His view challenges notions of free will and emphasizes the importance of understanding the underlying causes of events. Spinoza's deterministic perspective continues to provoke debate and exploration of the nature of human agency and the laws governing the universe.

May 23: Baruch Spinoza - Rational Understanding Leads to Happiness

B ARUCH SPINOZA BELIEVED THAT rational understanding and knowledge lead to true happiness and
freedom. In "Ethics," he argued that by understanding
the necessary causes of our emotions and actions, we can
achieve a state of intellectual love of God (amor intellectualis
Dei) and live in harmony with the natural order. This rational understanding liberates us from the passive emotions
that dominate our lives.

Spinoza used the example of overcoming fear to illustrate
this idea. He argued that understanding the causes of fear,
such as ignorance or superstition, allows us to rationally
address and mitigate it. By gaining knowledge and insight,
we can transform passive emotions into active emotions,
leading to greater autonomy and well-being.

Spinoza's emphasis on rational understanding as a path to
happiness resonates with modern cognitive and behavioral
therapies, which also focus on understanding and transforming emotions. His philosophy encourages the pursuit
of knowledge and self-awareness as keys to a fulfilled and
harmonious life, offering timeless insights into the human
quest for happiness.

May 24: John Locke - Tabula Rasa: Mind as a Blank Slate

J OHN LOCKE, AN ENGLISH philosopher, introduced the concept of "tabula rasa," which suggests that the mind is a blank slate at birth. According to Locke, all knowledge and ideas come from experience and sensory input. This theory was a radical departure from the prevailing notion of innate ideas and emphasized the importance of environment and education in shaping the human mind.

Locke used the example of a newborn child to illustrate tabula rasa. He argued that a child's mind is devoid of any knowledge or ideas at birth and that it acquires information through sensory experiences and reflection. This process of learning and knowledge accumulation continues throughout life, influenced by interactions with the external world.

Locke's tabula rasa theory had a profound impact on education and psychology, highlighting the importance of early childhood experiences and the environment in cognitive development. His ideas laid the groundwork for empiricism and influenced later thinkers, such as Jean-Jacques Rousseau and John Stuart Mill, who emphasized the role of experience in human development.

May 25: John Locke - Natural Rights: Life, Liberty, and Property

J OHN LOCKE IS ALSO known for his theory of natural rights, which asserts that individuals possess inherent rights to life, liberty, and property. Locke argued that these rights are fundamental and must be protected by any legitimate government. His ideas were grounded in the belief that individuals have the right to defend their own lives and property and to pursue their own happiness and freedom.

Locke used the example of property rights to illustrate his theory. He believed that individuals have the right to own property by mixing their labor with natural resources. For instance, cultivating a piece of land or creating a product establishes ownership over it. This right to property is crucial for individual autonomy and economic development.

Locke's theory of natural rights influenced the development of modern democratic principles and political philosophy. His ideas were instrumental in shaping the American Declaration of Independence and the Constitution, emphasizing the importance of individual rights and the role of government in protecting them.

May 26: John Locke - Government by Consent of the Governed

J OHN LOCKE'S POLITICAL PHILOSOPHY is centered on the idea that legitimate government arises from the consent of the governed. He argued that individuals form societies and governments through a social contract, agreeing to relinquish some of their freedoms in exchange for protection and the maintenance of order. This contract is based on mutual consent and can be revoked if the government fails to uphold its responsibilities.

Locke used the example of a civil society to explain this concept. He believed that in the state of nature, individuals have complete freedom but face constant threats to their security. By consenting to form a government, individuals collectively agree to create laws and institutions that protect their rights and promote the common good.

Locke's ideas on government by consent laid the foundation for modern democratic theory and influenced the development of constitutional government. His emphasis on the accountability of rulers and the right of the people to overthrow unjust governments has had a lasting impact on political thought and practice.

May 27: Gottfried Wilhelm Leibniz - Monadology

G OTTFRIED WILHELM LEIBNIZ, A German philosopher and mathematician, introduced the concept of
monadology, a metaphysical theory that posits that the universe is composed of simple, indivisible substances called
monads. Monads are the fundamental building blocks of
reality, each possessing unique properties and perceptions.
According to Leibniz, these monads do not interact directly
with each other but are harmonized by a pre-established
divine order.

Leibniz used the example of a clock to illustrate monadology. Just as each part of a clock operates independently but is
synchronized to produce a unified function, monads operate
independently but are coordinated by God's pre-established
harmony. This ensures that the universe functions in a coherent and orderly manner.

Leibniz's monadology challenged the mechanistic views of
his contemporaries, offering a more holistic and interconnected perspective on reality. His ideas influenced later
philosophical discussions on the nature of substance, perception, and the relationship between the individual and the
cosmos.

May 28: Gottfried Wilhelm Leibniz - Pre-established Harmony

L EIBNIZ'S THEORY OF PRE-ESTABLISHED harmony suggests that all monads in the universe are synchronized by God from the beginning of time. According to this theory, each monad follows its own internal principles and develops according to its own nature, but these developments are perfectly coordinated with those of other monads. This divine synchronization ensures a harmonious and orderly universe.

Leibniz used the analogy of two synchronized clocks to explain pre-established harmony. He argued that just as two clocks set to the same time will show the same time independently, monads are pre-programmed by God to harmonize with each other without direct interaction. This eliminates the need for causal interaction between monads while maintaining a coherent and functional universe.

Leibniz's concept of pre-established harmony addresses the problem of interaction between substances, offering a solution that emphasizes the role of a divine coordinator. His ideas have influenced subsequent philosophical and theological discussions on the nature of causality, determinism, and the relationship between God and the world.

May 29: Gottfried Wilhelm Leibniz - Best of All Possible Worlds

L EIBNIZ IS ALSO KNOWN for his optimistic philosophy, encapsulated in the idea that we live in the best of all possible worlds. He argued that, despite the presence of evil and suffering, God, being omnipotent and benevolent, has created the most optimal world possible. Leibniz believed that every event, good or bad, ultimately contributes to the greater good and the overall harmony of the universe.

Leibniz used the example of a complex tapestry to illustrate this idea. He compared the world to a tapestry, where individual threads (events) might seem disordered and unpleasant up close but contribute to a beautiful and coherent design when viewed as a whole. This perspective emphasizes the importance of considering the broader context when evaluating the nature of reality.

Leibniz's optimism has been both celebrated and critiqued, most notably by Voltaire in his satirical novel "Candide." Despite this, Leibniz's belief in the rationality and benevolence of the universe continues to influence philosophical and theological discussions on the nature of existence and the problem of evil.

May 30: Giambattista Vico - New Science: Cyclical Theory of History

G IAMBATTISTA VICO, AN ITALIAN philosopher and historian, introduced a cyclical theory of history in his work "The New Science." Vico argued that human history follows a recurring cycle of stages: the age of gods, the age of heroes, and the age of humans. Each stage represents a different mode of social organization and cultural expression, influenced by the collective mentality of the people.

Vico used the example of ancient civilizations to illustrate his cyclical theory. He observed that societies like ancient Greece and Rome evolved from religious and mythical origins (age of gods) to aristocratic and heroic societies (age of heroes), and finally to democratic and rational societies (age of humans). This pattern repeats as societies rise and fall, influenced by changing human consciousness.

Vico's cyclical theory of history challenged linear and progressive views of historical development. His work laid the foundation for later historical and sociological theories that emphasize the importance of cultural and psychological factors in shaping historical events. Vico's ideas continue to inspire scholars in the fields of history, anthropology, and philosophy.

MAY 31: GIAMBATTISTA VICO - VERUM IPSUM FACTUM: TRUTH IS MADE

V ICO INTRODUCED THE CONCEPT of "verum ipsum factum," which means "the true is precisely what is made." He argued that human knowledge is rooted in what humans create, and that understanding comes from engaging with and interpreting human-made artifacts, institutions, and practices. This perspective contrasts with the notion that truth is discovered through abstract reasoning or empirical observation alone.

Vico used the example of language to illustrate this idea. He believed that language is a human creation that reflects the collective consciousness and experiences of a society. By studying the evolution and use of language, one can gain insights into the nature of human thought and culture. This approach emphasizes the importance of history, literature, and art in understanding human knowledge.

Vico's concept of "verum ipsum factum" has influenced hermeneutics, the study of interpretation, and the philosophy of history. His ideas highlight the active role of human creativity in shaping knowledge and understanding, encouraging a more dynamic and interpretive approach to the study of human culture.

JUNE 1: GIAMBATTISTA VICO - IMAGINATION: ROLE IN HUMAN UNDERSTANDING

G IAMBATTISTA VICO ALSO EMPHASIZED the role of imagination in human understanding. He believed that imagination is a fundamental aspect of human cognition, enabling individuals to create myths, symbols, and narratives that shape their perception of the world. Vico argued that imagination allows people to make sense of complex and abstract concepts by transforming them into concrete and relatable forms.

Vico used the example of mythology to illustrate the importance of imagination. He observed that early societies used myths and legends to explain natural phenomena and social norms, imbuing them with meaning and significance. These imaginative constructs provided a framework for understanding the world and guiding human behavior.

Vico's emphasis on imagination has influenced subsequent philosophical and psychological theories, particularly in the fields of phenomenology and existentialism. His ideas underscore the creative and interpretive dimensions of human knowledge, highlighting the importance of imagination in shaping cultural and individual understanding.

JUNE 2: THOMAS REID - COMMON SENSE PHILOSOPHY

T HOMAS REID, A SCOTTISH philosopher, is known for founding the school of Common Sense Philosophy. Reid argued that common sense beliefs—those that are universally accepted and intuitively obvious—form the foundation of human knowledge. He believed that skepticism about these basic beliefs leads to absurd conclusions and that common sense should guide philosophical inquiry.

Reid used the example of perception to illustrate his philosophy. He argued that our sensory experiences provide us with direct and reliable knowledge of the external world. For instance, seeing a tree in front of us is sufficient evidence of its existence. Doubting such basic perceptions undermines the practical functioning of everyday life.

Reid's Common Sense Philosophy was a response to the skepticism of David Hume and the idealism of George Berkeley. His emphasis on the reliability of common sense beliefs influenced later philosophers, including G.E. Moore and the American pragmatists. Reid's work underscores the importance of grounding philosophical inquiry in the intuitive and practical aspects of human experience.

JUNE 3: THOMAS REID - DIRECT REALISM

T HOMAS REID ALSO ADVOCATED for direct realism, the view that we perceive the world directly as it is, without any intermediary representations or ideas. According to Reid, our sensory experiences provide us with immediate access to the external world, and these experiences are generally accurate reflections of reality.

Reid used the example of visual perception to support direct realism. He argued that when we see an object, such as a chair, we are directly aware of the chair itself, not an internal image or idea of the chair. This direct awareness provides us with reliable knowledge of the object's properties and existence.

Reid's direct realism challenged the representational theories of perception proposed by philosophers like René Descartes and John Locke. His emphasis on the directness and reliability of sensory perception has influenced contemporary discussions in the philosophy of mind and epistemology, supporting a more straightforward approach to understanding human cognition and the nature of reality.

June 4: Thomas Reid - Moral Sense

T HOMAS REID IS ALSO known for his theory of moral
sense, which posits that humans have an innate ability
to perceive moral truths, similar to how they perceive physical objects. Reid believed that moral judgments are grounded in this natural faculty, allowing individuals to distinguish
between right and wrong intuitively.

Reid used the example of empathy to illustrate moral sense.
He argued that when we observe someone in distress, our
immediate emotional response reflects an inherent understanding of their suffering and a recognition of our moral
duty to help. This intuitive grasp of moral principles guides
our ethical behavior and decision-making.

Reid's theory of moral sense influenced later philosophers,
including the Scottish Enlightenment thinkers and moral
philosophers like Adam Smith. His emphasis on the innate
and intuitive aspects of moral perception highlights the natural foundations of ethical judgment and the role of human
nature in shaping moral understanding.

June 5: David Hume - Empiricism: Knowledge from Experience

D AVID HUME, A SCOTTISH philosopher, is a central figure in the development of empiricism, the theory that all knowledge is derived from sensory experience. Hume argued that human understanding is limited to what can be observed and experienced, and that abstract reasoning alone cannot provide knowledge about the world. This emphasis on experience as the basis for knowledge challenges rationalist views that prioritize innate ideas and deductive reasoning.

Hume used the example of cause and effect to illustrate empiricism. He argued that our understanding of causation is based on the observation of repeated associations between events, rather than any inherent logical connection. For instance, seeing that pressing a light switch consistently turns on a light leads us to infer a causal relationship, but this inference is grounded in experience, not reason.

Hume's empiricism has had a profound impact on the philosophy of science and epistemology, influencing later thinkers like Immanuel Kant and the logical positivists. His work underscores the importance of observation and experience in acquiring knowledge and shaping our understanding of the world.

June 6: David Hume - Skepticism: Questioning Certainty of Knowledge

D AVID HUME IS ALSO known for his skeptical approach to philosophy, particularly his questioning of the certainty of knowledge. Hume argued that many of our beliefs, especially those about causation, the self, and the external world, lack rational justification and are based on habit and custom rather than logical proof. His skepticism challenges the assumption that human reason can achieve absolute certainty.

Hume used the example of induction to illustrate his skepticism. He pointed out that while we routinely infer general principles from specific observations (e.g., the sun will rise tomorrow because it has always risen in the past), there is no logical basis for assuming that the future will always resemble the past. This problem of induction highlights the limits of empirical reasoning and the uncertainty underlying many of our beliefs.

Hume's skepticism has influenced a wide range of philosophical discussions, from the philosophy of science to metaphysics. His work encourages a critical examination of the foundations of knowledge and highlights the provisional nature of many of our beliefs.

June 7: David Hume - Problem of Induction

D AVID HUME'S ANALYSIS OF the problem of induction is one of his most significant contributions to philosophy. The problem of induction concerns the justification of inferences from specific observations to general conclusions. Hume argued that there is no rational basis for assuming that the future will resemble the past, and thus, all inductive reasoning is ultimately unjustified.

Hume used the example of predicting the sunrise to illustrate this problem. While we expect the sun to rise every morning based on past experience, there is no logical necessity that guarantees this pattern will continue. This expectation is a matter of habit, not rational certainty, and highlights the fundamental uncertainty in our empirical beliefs.

The problem of induction has had a lasting impact on the philosophy of science and epistemology, prompting debates on the nature of scientific reasoning and the justification of empirical knowledge. Hume's analysis challenges us to reconsider the assumptions underlying our understanding of the world and the limits of human knowledge.

June 8: Jean-Jacques Rousseau - Social Contract: General Will

J EAN-JACQUES ROUSSEAU, A FRENCH philosopher, is best known for his work on the social contract and the concept of the general will. Rousseau argued that individuals enter into a social contract to form a collective body politic, where the general will represents the common interests of all citizens. This general will is not merely the sum of individual desires but a unified, collective will that aims for the common good.

Rousseau used the example of a democratic assembly to illustrate the general will. In such an assembly, individuals set aside their personal interests to deliberate and decide on laws and policies that benefit the entire community. The general will emerges from this collective decision-making process, reflecting the shared values and goals of the society.

Rousseau's ideas on the social contract and the general will have influenced modern democratic theory and political philosophy. His emphasis on collective decision-making and the common good challenges individualistic perspectives and highlights the importance of civic responsibility and participation in governance.

June 9: Jean-Jacques Rousseau - Noble Savage: Natural Goodness of Humans

R OUSSEAU IS ALSO KNOWN for his concept of the "noble savage," which suggests that humans are inherently good and that society corrupts this natural goodness. He believed that in their natural state, humans are compassionate, self-sufficient, and live in harmony with nature. It is the constraints and inequalities of civilization that lead to selfishness, competition, and moral decay.

Rousseau used the example of indigenous peoples to illustrate the noble savage. He argued that indigenous societies, living closer to nature and without the complexities of modern civilization, often exhibit qualities of cooperation, empathy, and simplicity. These societies contrast sharply with the corruption and vice seen in more developed civilizations.

Rousseau's romanticized view of the noble savage has influenced various fields, including anthropology, literature, and political thought. His ideas challenge the assumption that progress and civilization inherently lead to moral improvement, prompting a re-evaluation of the relationship between nature, society, and human goodness.

June 10: Jean-Jacques Rousseau - Education Should Nurture Rather Than Impose

R OUSSEAU'S EDUCATIONAL PHILOSOPHY, PARTICU-
LARLY articulated in his work "Emile," emphasizes
that education should nurture the natural development of
children rather than impose rigid structures and knowledge.
He believed that children learn best through experiences
and interactions with their environment, allowing their innate curiosity and abilities to flourish.

Rousseau used the example of gardening to illustrate his
educational philosophy. Just as a gardener provides the necessary conditions for plants to grow according to their nature, educators should create an environment that fosters
the natural growth and development of children. This approach encourages learning through exploration and discovery, rather than rote memorization and strict discipline.

Rousseau's ideas on education have had a lasting impact
on modern educational theory and practice. His emphasis
on child-centered learning, experiential education, and the
importance of fostering natural development continues to
influence progressive education movements and approaches to teaching and learning.

June 11: Jean le Rond d'Alembert - Encyclopédie: Compilation of Human Knowledge

JEAN LE ROND D'ALEMBERT, a French philosopher, mathematician, and co-editor of the "Encyclopédie," aimed to compile and disseminate human knowledge across various fields. The "Encyclopédie" was a monumental work that sought to promote enlightenment ideals, including reason, science, and secularism, by making knowledge accessible to a broader audience.

D'Alembert used the example of the scientific method to highlight the importance of the "Encyclopédie." By including detailed entries on scientific principles and discoveries, the work aimed to educate and inform the public, encouraging critical thinking and intellectual curiosity. This comprehensive compilation reflected the Enlightenment's commitment to knowledge and progress.

The "Encyclopédie" had a profound impact on the dissemination of knowledge and the promotion of Enlightenment ideals. It played a crucial role in shaping modern intellectual and cultural landscapes, influencing subsequent encyclopedic works and the development of educational resources.

June 12: Jean le Rond d'Alembert - Materialism: Physical Matter as the Basis of Reality

D'ALEMBERT WAS ALSO A proponent of materialism, the philosophical view that physical matter is the fundamental substance of reality. He argued that all phenomena, including mental and spiritual experiences, can be explained through physical processes and interactions. This perspective challenged dualistic and idealistic views that posited a separate, non-material realm.

D'Alembert used the example of human consciousness to illustrate materialism. He believed that consciousness arises from the complex interactions of physical processes in the brain, rather than from an immaterial soul. This view aligns with scientific approaches to understanding the mind and rejects supernatural explanations.

Materialism, as advocated by d'Alembert, has influenced various scientific and philosophical disciplines. It underscores the importance of empirical investigation and the search for natural explanations of phenomena, contributing to the development of modern science and the rejection of metaphysical speculations.

June 13: Jean le Rond d'Alembert - Skepticism: Questioning Religious Dogma

D'ALEMBERT WAS KNOWN FOR his skepticism, particularly in questioning religious dogma and traditional beliefs. He advocated for a rational and critical approach to understanding the world, challenging the authority of religious institutions and doctrines that lacked empirical evidence and logical coherence.

D'Alembert used the example of miracles to illustrate his skepticism. He argued that miraculous claims, often used to support religious beliefs, should be subjected to rigorous scrutiny and empirical testing. Without reliable evidence, such claims should be regarded with skepticism and not taken as proof of divine intervention.

D'Alembert's skeptical approach contributed to the broader Enlightenment critique of religion and the promotion of secularism. His emphasis on reason and evidence over faith and tradition has influenced modern atheism, agnosticism, and the scientific worldview, encouraging a critical examination of all claims to knowledge.

JUNE 14: IMMANUEL KANT - CATEGORICAL IMPERATIVE

I MMANUEL KANT, A GERMAN philosopher, introduced the concept of the categorical imperative, a central element of his moral philosophy. The categorical imperative is a universal moral law that applies to all rational beings, regardless of personal desires or circumstances. Kant argued that moral actions must be guided by principles that can be consistently applied to everyone.

Kant used the example of lying to illustrate the categorical imperative. He argued that if lying were universally acceptable, trust and communication would break down, making it impossible to function in society. Therefore, lying cannot be morally justified because it cannot be universalized without contradiction. The categorical imperative requires individuals to act according to maxims that can be consistently willed as universal laws.

Kant's categorical imperative has had a profound impact on ethical theory, emphasizing the importance of duty, intention, and universalizability in moral decision-making. His ideas continue to influence contemporary debates in ethics, particularly deontological approaches that prioritize principles over consequences.

June 15: Immanuel Kant - Phenomena vs. Noumena

I MMANUEL KANT'S DISTINCTION BETWEEN phenomena and noumena is a key aspect of his epistemology. According to Kant, phenomena are the objects of our sensory experience, which we can perceive and understand through our cognitive faculties. Noumena, on the other hand, are things as they exist in themselves, independent of our perception, which we cannot directly know or experience.

Kant used the example of a tree to explain this distinction. The tree as we perceive it—its color, shape, and texture—is a phenomenon. However, the tree as it exists in itself, beyond our sensory and cognitive faculties, is a noumenon. Kant argued that our knowledge is limited to phenomena, and we can never have direct access to the noumenal reality.

Kant's distinction between phenomena and noumena has influenced various fields, including metaphysics, epistemology, and the philosophy of science. It highlights the limits of human knowledge and the role of our cognitive structures in shaping our experience of the world. This perspective has prompted ongoing debates about the nature of reality and the scope of human understanding.

June 16: Immanuel Kant - Autonomy: Self-imposed Moral Law

K ANT'S CONCEPT OF AUTONOMY is central to his moral philosophy, emphasizing the idea that individuals are bound by self-imposed moral laws. Autonomy, for Kant, means acting according to principles that one has rationally determined and accepted as binding. This self-governance reflects the capacity of rational agents to legislate moral laws for themselves, independent of external influences.

Kant used the example of moral duty to illustrate autonomy. He argued that a person who helps others out of genuine moral duty, rather than for personal gain or external reward, exemplifies autonomy. Such actions are guided by a respect for the moral law that the individual has rationally recognized and adopted.

Kant's emphasis on autonomy has had a significant impact on modern ethical theory, particularly in discussions of moral responsibility, freedom, and dignity. His ideas underscore the importance of rational deliberation and self-legislation in ethical behavior, influencing contemporary debates on personal autonomy and the foundations of moral principles.

June 17: Edmund Burke - Conservatism: Value of Tradition

E DMUND BURKE, AN IRISH statesman and philosopher, is often regarded as the father of modern conservatism. Burke emphasized the value of tradition and the accumulated wisdom of past generations in guiding society. He believed that social institutions and customs evolve over time to address the complexities of human life and should be preserved and respected.

Burke used the example of the British monarchy to illustrate his conservative principles. He argued that the monarchy, as an enduring institution, provides stability and continuity, embodying the historical and cultural identity of the nation. Sudden and radical changes, according to Burke, risk undermining this stability and the societal order.

Burke's conservatism has influenced political thought and practice, advocating for gradual and cautious reform rather than revolutionary change. His emphasis on tradition, continuity, and the prudence of inherited practices remains a cornerstone of conservative ideology, shaping debates on social and political change.

JUNE 18: EDMUND BURKE - SUBLIME AND BEAUTIFUL: AESTHETIC THEORIES

E DMUND BURKE ALSO MADE significant contributions to aesthetics, particularly through his distinction between the sublime and the beautiful. In his work "A Philosophical Enquiry into the Origin of Our Ideas of the Sublime and Beautiful," Burke explored how different experiences of nature and art evoke distinct emotional responses. The sublime is associated with awe and terror, while the beautiful is linked to harmony and pleasure.

Burke used the example of a vast, towering mountain to illustrate the sublime. The mountain's sheer size and grandeur inspire a sense of awe and insignificance, triggering a profound emotional response. In contrast, a well-proportioned garden, with its orderly and pleasing arrangement, exemplifies the beautiful, evoking a sense of calm and enjoyment.

Burke's aesthetic theories have influenced the study of art, literature, and psychology, shaping our understanding of emotional responses to different forms of beauty and grandeur. His work highlights the complexity of aesthetic experience and the diverse ways in which humans interact with their environment.

June 19: Edmund Burke - Critique of the French Revolution

E DMUND BURKE IS WELL-KNOWN for his critique of the French Revolution, which he articulated in his work "Reflections on the Revolution in France." Burke argued that the revolution's radical and violent methods threatened the social fabric and the stability of society. He believed that the revolutionaries' disregard for tradition and established institutions would lead to chaos and tyranny.

Burke used the example of the French monarchy's fall to illustrate his concerns. He saw the execution of King Louis XVI and the dismantling of long-standing institutions as a reckless break from the past, leading to unpredictable and dangerous outcomes. Burke advocated for reform within existing structures, rather than revolutionary upheaval.

Burke's critique of the French Revolution has had a lasting impact on political theory, reinforcing conservative arguments for gradual change and the preservation of social order. His emphasis on prudence, tradition, and the potential dangers of radicalism continues to resonate in contemporary political discourse.

June 20: Mary Wollstonecraft - Women's Rights: Education and Equality

MARY WOLLSTONECRAFT, AN ENGLISH writer and philosopher, is a pioneering advocate for women's rights, particularly in the areas of education and equality. In her seminal work "A Vindication of the Rights of Woman," Wollstonecraft argued that women are not naturally inferior to men but appear so only because they lack access to education. She believed that educating women would enable them to contribute equally to society and achieve true independence.

Wollstonecraft used the example of domestic roles to illustrate her point. She argued that women, confined to domestic duties and denied educational opportunities, are unable to develop their full potential. By providing equal education, women could pursue careers, engage in intellectual activities, and participate fully in public life.

Wollstonecraft's advocacy for women's rights and education has had a profound impact on feminist thought and the broader movement for gender equality. Her work continues to inspire efforts to improve educational opportunities for women and to challenge societal norms that limit women's roles and achievements.

June 21: Mary Wollstonecraft - Rationalism: Women's Rational Capacity

M ARY WOLLSTONECRAFT EMPHASIZED THE importance of rationalism and the intellectual capabilities of women. She argued that women possess the same capacity for reason as men and should be encouraged to develop their minds through education and intellectual pursuits. Wollstonecraft believed that recognizing women's rational abilities would lead to more equitable and just societies.

Wollstonecraft used the example of intellectual debate to illustrate women's rational capacity. She argued that women, when given the opportunity to engage in philosophical and scientific discussions, demonstrate equal aptitude and critical thinking skills as men. This potential is often unrealized due to societal constraints and lack of access to education.

Wollstonecraft's focus on rationalism and equality challenged the prevailing views of her time, which often portrayed women as inherently emotional and irrational. Her work laid the groundwork for modern feminist philosophy, advocating for the recognition of women's intellectual and rational capabilities and their equal participation in all areas of life.

June 22: Mary Wollstonecraft - Empowered Motherhood for a Better Society

M ARY WOLLSTONECRAFT ALSO HIGHLIGHTED the role of empowered motherhood in creating a better society. She believed that well-educated and independent mothers would raise children who are more thoughtful, responsible, and capable citizens. Wollstonecraft argued that empowering women through education and social equality would have far-reaching benefits for families and society as a whole.

Wollstonecraft used the example of parenting to illustrate the impact of empowered motherhood. She argued that mothers who are educated and respected are better equipped to teach their children values, critical thinking, and social responsibility. This, in turn, fosters a more enlightened and virtuous society.

Wollstonecraft's vision of empowered motherhood remains relevant today, influencing discussions on parenting, education, and gender equality. Her ideas continue to inspire efforts to support and empower women, recognizing the pivotal role they play in shaping future generations and contributing to the betterment of society.

JUNE 23: G.W.F. HEGEL - DIALECTICS: THESIS, ANTITHESIS, SYNTHESIS

GEORG WILHELM FRIEDRICH HEGEL, a German philosopher, is known for his dialectical method, which involves the process of thesis, antithesis, and synthesis. This method describes the progression of ideas and reality through a dynamic and conflict-driven process. According to Hegel, every idea (thesis) inevitably encounters its opposite (antithesis), and their resolution leads to a higher level of understanding (synthesis).

Hegel used the example of historical development to illustrate dialectics. He believed that each historical period contains contradictions that lead to its eventual transformation. For instance, the Enlightenment's emphasis on reason (thesis) was challenged by Romanticism's focus on emotion (antithesis), resulting in a new cultural synthesis that integrated elements of both.

Hegel's dialectical method has had a significant impact on various fields, including philosophy, history, and political theory. It influenced later thinkers like Karl Marx and Friedrich Engels, who adapted Hegelian dialectics to their materialist conception of history. Hegel's approach emphasizes the dynamic and evolutionary nature of reality and ideas, highlighting the importance of conflict and resolution in progress.

June 24: G.W.F. Hegel - Absolute Spirit: Ultimate Reality and Truth

H EGEL'S CONCEPT OF THE Absolute Spirit represents the culmination of his philosophical system, where ultimate reality and truth are realized. The Absolute Spirit is the totality of existence, encompassing both the material and spiritual dimensions. Hegel believed that the Absolute Spirit manifests itself through history, culture, and individual consciousness, ultimately achieving self-awareness and unity.

Hegel used the example of art, religion, and philosophy to illustrate the development of the Absolute Spirit. He argued that these cultural forms represent different stages of the Spirit's self-realization. Art expresses the Spirit through sensory forms, religion through symbolic representations, and philosophy through rational thought. The progression from art to philosophy reflects the increasing clarity and self-awareness of the Absolute Spirit.

Hegel's notion of the Absolute Spirit influenced later existentialist and phenomenological thinkers, who explored the nature of human consciousness and its relationship to reality. His ideas underscore the interconnectedness of all aspects of existence and the unfolding of truth through a dialectical process.

June 25: G.W.F. Hegel - History as a Rational Process

H EGEL VIEWED HISTORY AS a rational process driven by the unfolding of the World Spirit, which he believed guides the development of human societies and cultures towards greater freedom and self-awareness. According to Hegel, history is not a random sequence of events but a coherent and purposeful progression that reflects the dialectical development of ideas and institutions.

Hegel used the example of the evolution of political systems to illustrate this rational process. He argued that each stage of political development, from ancient despotism to modern democracy, represents a step towards the realization of human freedom. The conflicts and contradictions within each system drive the historical process forward, leading to higher forms of social organization.

Hegel's interpretation of history as a rational process has influenced various schools of thought, including Marxism and existentialism. His emphasis on the teleological nature of history challenges purely empirical and materialist views, suggesting that historical events are part of a broader, meaningful trajectory.

June 26: Arthur Schopenhauer - Will to Live: Fundamental Force

ARTHUR SCHOPENHAUER, A GERMAN philosopher, introduced the concept of the "Will to Live" as the fundamental force driving all existence. According to Schopenhauer, the Will is an irrational, blind, and insatiable drive that underlies all human desires, actions, and natural processes. This Will manifests in individuals as a relentless striving for survival and reproduction.

Schopenhauer used the example of human desires to illustrate the Will to Live. He argued that our desires and actions are ultimately motivated by this underlying Will, which seeks to perpetuate life at all costs. This drive is not rational but an inherent aspect of our being, influencing our behavior and decisions.

Schopenhauer's concept of the Will to Live contrasts with the rationalist and idealist philosophies of his time. His focus on the irrational and unconscious aspects of human nature influenced later existentialist and psychoanalytic thinkers, such as Friedrich Nietzsche and Sigmund Freud. Schopenhauer's ideas highlight the fundamental and often conflictual nature of human existence.

June 27: Arthur Schopenhauer - Pessimism: Life is Suffering

S CHOPENHAUER IS ALSO KNOWN for his philosophical pessimism, which posits that life is characterized by suffering and dissatisfaction. He believed that the insatiable Will to Live condemns individuals to a constant state of striving and yearning, leading to inevitable frustration and pain. According to Schopenhauer, the pursuit of desires only provides temporary relief, as new desires and needs continually arise.

Schopenhauer used the example of the hedonic treadmill to explain his pessimism. He argued that achieving a desired goal provides only fleeting satisfaction before new desires emerge, perpetuating a cycle of unfulfilled striving. This relentless pursuit of desires leads to suffering and a sense of futility.

Schopenhauer's pessimism has had a significant impact on existentialist and modernist literature, as well as on the philosophy of suffering. His ideas challenge optimistic and progressivist views, emphasizing the intrinsic difficulties of human existence and the importance of recognizing and addressing suffering.

JUNE 28: ARTHUR SCHOPENHAUER - AESTHETICS: ART AS AN ESCAPE

DESPITE HIS PESSIMISTIC OUTLOOK, Schopenhauer believed that art offers a temporary escape from the suffering of life. He argued that aesthetic experiences allow individuals to transcend their individual Will and enter a state of contemplation and detachment. In this state, one can appreciate beauty and harmony without being driven by personal desires and anxieties.

Schopenhauer used the example of music to illustrate the power of art. He believed that music, more than any other art form, provides a direct expression of the Will and allows listeners to experience a sense of unity and peace. Through music, individuals can momentarily transcend their personal struggles and connect with a deeper, universal reality.

Schopenhauer's aesthetics have influenced various artists, writers, and musicians, including Richard Wagner and Thomas Mann. His ideas underscore the therapeutic and transformative potential of art, highlighting its role in providing relief from the burdens of existence and offering glimpses of a more profound reality.

June 29: Auguste Comte - Positivism: Empirical Sciences

AUGUSTE COMTE, A FRENCH philosopher and sociologist, is known for developing positivism, a philosophical approach that emphasizes the importance of empirical sciences in understanding the world. Comte argued that knowledge should be based on observable phenomena and scientific inquiry, rejecting metaphysical and theological explanations.

Comte used the example of the natural sciences to illustrate positivism. He believed that disciplines like physics, chemistry, and biology provide reliable knowledge through systematic observation, experimentation, and verification. By applying the scientific method to all areas of inquiry, including social sciences, Comte aimed to establish a comprehensive and unified understanding of reality.

Comte's positivism has had a lasting impact on the development of modern science and sociology. His emphasis on empirical evidence and scientific methodology continues to influence research practices and the pursuit of knowledge across various fields.

JUNE 30: AUGUSTE COMTE - LAW OF THREE STAGES

C OMTE PROPOSED THE "LAW of Three Stages" as a framework for understanding the evolution of human thought and society. According to this theory, human knowledge and society progress through three distinct stages: the theological, the metaphysical, and the positive (scientific). Each stage represents a different mode of explaining and organizing the world.

Comte used the example of explanations for natural phenomena to illustrate the three stages. In the theological stage, phenomena are attributed to supernatural beings or deities. In the metaphysical stage, abstract principles and forces replace supernatural explanations. Finally, in the positive stage, scientific inquiry and empirical observation provide natural and verifiable explanations for phenomena.

Comte's Law of Three Stages has influenced the study of intellectual history and the development of sociology. His framework emphasizes the progression towards scientific understanding and the increasing reliance on empirical methods in explaining the world.

July 1: Auguste Comte - Sociology: Scientific Study of Society

A UGUSTE COMTE IS ALSO known for founding sociology as a distinct academic discipline. He believed that society should be studied scientifically, using empirical methods to understand social phenomena and develop solutions to social problems. Comte's vision for sociology involved applying the principles of positivism to the study of social structures, institutions, and relationships.

Comte used the example of social order and progress to illustrate the goals of sociology. He argued that by scientifically analyzing the factors that contribute to social stability and change, sociologists can develop strategies to improve societal well-being and address issues such as inequality, conflict, and social cohesion.

Comte's establishment of sociology as a scientific discipline has had a profound impact on the study of society. His emphasis on empirical research and the application of scientific methods to social issues continues to shape contemporary sociology and inform efforts to understand and address complex social challenges.

July 2: Ralph Waldo Emerson - Self-Reliance

R ALPH WALDO EMERSON, AN American transcendentalist philosopher and writer, is best known for his
essay "Self-Reliance." In this work, Emerson advocates for
individualism and personal independence, urging people to
trust their inner voice and intuition rather than conform
to societal expectations and external authority. He believed
that true fulfillment and greatness come from within.

Emerson used the example of nonconformity to illustrate
self-reliance. He argued that individuals should resist the
pressure to conform to social norms and instead follow
their own path, even if it leads to isolation or criticism. By
being true to oneself and embracing one's unique talents
and insights, individuals can achieve personal growth and
contribute authentically to society.

Emerson's emphasis on self-reliance has had a lasting impact on American thought and culture, influencing figures
such as Henry David Thoreau and Walt Whitman. His ideas
continue to inspire the pursuit of personal authenticity, creativity, and independence.

July 3: Ralph Waldo Emerson - The Oversoul

E MERSON'S CONCEPT OF THE Oversoul is central to his transcendentalist philosophy. He believed that the Oversoul is a universal spirit that connects all individuals and the natural world. According to Emerson, this divine presence transcends individual consciousness and unites humanity in a shared spiritual experience.

Emerson used the example of nature to illustrate the Oversoul. He argued that by immersing oneself in nature, one can experience a sense of unity and connection with the larger cosmos. This transcendent experience reveals the interconnectedness of all life and the presence of the divine in everyday existence.

Emerson's notion of the Oversoul has influenced various spiritual and philosophical traditions, emphasizing the importance of inner experience and the unity of all beings. His ideas encourage a holistic and spiritual perspective on life, highlighting the interconnectedness of individuals and the natural world.

July 4: Ralph Waldo Emerson - Nature as a Source of Inspiration

R ALPH WALDO EMERSON VIEWED nature as a profound source of inspiration and wisdom. In his essay "Nature," he explores the idea that the natural world offers insights into the human spirit and serves as a reflection of the divine. Emerson believed that by connecting with nature, individuals can gain clarity, creativity, and a deeper understanding of themselves and the universe.

Emerson used the example of the changing seasons to illustrate the inspirational power of nature. He argued that the cyclical patterns of growth, decay, and renewal in nature mirror the human experience and provide a sense of continuity and purpose. Observing these natural processes can inspire creativity and a sense of harmony with the world.

Emerson's reverence for nature has influenced environmental thought and the appreciation of the natural world in literature and philosophy. His ideas continue to inspire individuals to seek solace and inspiration in nature, fostering a deeper connection with the environment and a greater sense of ecological responsibility.

July 5: John Stuart Mill - Utilitarianism: Greatest Happiness Principle

J OHN STUART MILL, A British philosopher and economist, is a key figure in the development of utilitarianism,
an ethical theory that advocates for actions that promote the
greatest happiness for the greatest number of people. Mill
refined and expanded upon the utilitarian ideas of Jeremy
Bentham, emphasizing the quality of pleasures and the importance of individual rights.

Mill used the example of moral decision-making to illustrate utilitarianism. He argued that when faced with a moral
dilemma, individuals should consider the consequences of
their actions and choose the option that maximizes overall
happiness and minimizes suffering. This principle provides
a practical and flexible framework for evaluating ethical
choices.

Mill's utilitarianism has had a significant impact on moral
philosophy and public policy, influencing debates on issues
such as justice, welfare, and human rights. His emphasis on
the balance between individual happiness and the greater
good continues to shape ethical theory and practice.

July 6: John Stuart Mill - Liberty: Protection of Individual Freedom

J OHN STUART MILL IS also renowned for his defense of individual liberty, articulated in his essay "On Liberty." Mill argued that individuals should have the freedom to pursue their own interests and make their own choices, as long as their actions do not harm others. He believed that personal freedom is essential for individual development and social progress.

Mill used the example of freedom of speech to illustrate the importance of liberty. He argued that allowing diverse opinions and open debate fosters a more informed and dynamic society. Censorship, on the other hand, stifles intellectual growth and impedes the discovery of truth. Mill's "harm principle" asserts that the only justification for restricting individual liberty is to prevent harm to others.

Mill's advocacy for individual liberty has had a lasting influence on liberal political theory and human rights. His ideas continue to inform discussions on personal freedom, autonomy, and the role of government in protecting and promoting individual rights.

July 7: John Stuart Mill - Advocacy for Gender Equality

J OHN STUART MILL WAS a strong advocate for gender equality and women's rights, as evidenced in his work "The Subjection of Women." Mill argued that women should have the same legal and social rights as men, including the right to education, employment, and political participation. He believed that gender equality would lead to a more just and prosperous society.

Mill used the example of women's suffrage to illustrate his advocacy for gender equality. He argued that denying women the right to vote was an unjust restriction of their liberty and a barrier to social progress. By granting women equal rights and opportunities, society could benefit from their talents, perspectives, and contributions.

Mill's advocacy for gender equality has had a significant impact on the feminist movement and the struggle for women's rights. His ideas continue to inspire efforts to achieve gender equality and challenge discriminatory practices and laws.

JULY 8: CHARLES DARWIN - NATURAL SELECTION

C HARLES DARWIN, AN ENGLISH naturalist, revolutionized biology with his theory of natural selection. In his groundbreaking work "On the Origin of Species," Darwin proposed that species evolve over time through a process of natural selection, where individuals with advantageous traits are more likely to survive and reproduce. This process leads to the gradual adaptation of species to their environments.

Darwin used the example of finches on the Galápagos Islands to illustrate natural selection. He observed that finches with different beak shapes were better suited to different types of food. Over time, these variations led to the emergence of distinct species, each adapted to its specific ecological niche. This observation supported his theory that natural selection drives evolutionary change.

Darwin's theory of natural selection has had a profound impact on biology, shaping our understanding of the diversity of life and the mechanisms of evolution. His ideas continue to influence scientific research and have broader implications for fields such as genetics, ecology, and anthropology.

July 9: Charles Darwin - Common Descent

C HARLES DARWIN'S THEORY OF common descent posits that all living organisms share a common ancestor and that the diversity of life results from the branching evolutionary process. This idea is central to Darwin's evolutionary theory and provides a unifying framework for understanding the relationships between different species.

Darwin used the example of the tree of life to illustrate common descent. He envisioned the history of life as a branching tree, where each branch represents a lineage that diverges from common ancestors. Fossil evidence, comparative anatomy, and embryology all support the idea of common descent, showing the connections between seemingly disparate species.

Darwin's concept of common descent has revolutionized our understanding of biological diversity and the interconnectedness of all life forms. It forms the basis of modern evolutionary biology and continues to guide research in fields such as genetics, paleontology, and systematics.

July 10: Charles Darwin - Adaptation of Species

C HARLES DARWIN ALSO EMPHASIZED the role of adaptation in the evolution of species. According to Darwin, natural selection drives the development of adaptations—traits that enhance an organism's survival and reproductive success in its environment. These adaptations result from variations that arise through genetic mutations and are favored by natural selection.

Darwin used the example of the peppered moth to illustrate adaptation. During the Industrial Revolution in England, pollution darkened tree trunks, making dark-colored moths less visible to predators compared to their lighter counterparts. This led to an increase in the population of dark-colored moths, an example of adaptation to changing environmental conditions.

Darwin's insights into adaptation have had a lasting impact on our understanding of evolutionary processes. His ideas continue to inform research on how species respond to environmental changes, providing a framework for studying biodiversity, conservation, and the effects of climate change on living organisms.

JULY 11: SØREN KIERKEGAARD - SUBJECTIVITY AS TRUTH

S ØREN KIERKEGAARD, A DANISH philosopher, is considered the father of existentialism. He emphasized the importance of individual experience and personal perspective, encapsulated in his idea that "subjectivity is truth." Kierkegaard argued that objective truths, such as scientific facts, are different from subjective truths, which pertain to personal beliefs, emotions, and choices.

Kierkegaard used the example of religious faith to illustrate subjectivity. He believed that faith is a deeply personal experience that cannot be fully explained or justified by objective evidence. For Kierkegaard, the truth of one's faith lies in the sincerity and commitment of the individual believer, not in empirical verification.

Kierkegaard's focus on subjectivity has influenced existentialist thinkers like Jean-Paul Sartre and Martin Heidegger. His ideas underscore the importance of personal authenticity and the unique perspectives each individual brings to their understanding of the world, challenging the notion that objective truth is the only valid form of knowledge.

July 12: Søren Kierkegaard - The Leap of Faith

K IERKEGAARD IS ALSO KNOWN for his concept of the "leap of faith," which describes the act of embracing religious belief despite the absence of rational evidence or certainty. He believed that true faith requires a personal commitment that goes beyond reason, involving a leap into the unknown driven by passion and conviction.

Kierkegaard used the story of Abraham and Isaac to illustrate the leap of faith. According to the biblical narrative, Abraham's willingness to sacrifice his son Isaac, based solely on his faith in God's command, exemplifies a profound and irrational commitment. For Kierkegaard, this act represents the ultimate leap of faith, transcending ethical and logical considerations.

The leap of faith has resonated with existentialist and religious philosophers, highlighting the tension between reason and faith. Kierkegaard's concept encourages individuals to confront the uncertainties of existence and make deeply personal commitments, even in the face of doubt and ambiguity.

July 13: Søren Kierkegaard - The Three Stages of Life: Aesthetic, Ethical, Religious

K IERKEGAARD IDENTIFIED THREE STAGES of life through which individuals progress: the aesthetic, the ethical, and the religious. Each stage represents a different approach to living and understanding existence. The aesthetic stage focuses on personal pleasure and sensory experiences, the ethical stage emphasizes moral responsibility and social norms, and the religious stage involves a personal relationship with the divine.

Kierkegaard used the example of a hedonist to illustrate the aesthetic stage. This person seeks immediate gratification and avoids commitments, leading to a shallow and ultimately unfulfilling life. Transitioning to the ethical stage, an individual starts to consider the impact of their actions on others and adheres to societal rules and duties.

Finally, in the religious stage, Kierkegaard argued that individuals transcend societal norms and find true meaning through a personal connection with God. This stage requires embracing faith and accepting the paradoxes and uncertainties of religious belief. Kierkegaard's three stages of life offer a framework for understanding human development and the search for purpose.

July 14: Henry David Thoreau - Civil Disobedience

H ENRY DAVID THOREAU, AN American transcendentalist philosopher and writer, is best known for his
essay "Civil Disobedience." In this work, Thoreau argues
that individuals have a moral duty to resist unjust laws and
government actions through nonviolent resistance. He believed that personal conscience should guide one's actions,
even if it means breaking the law.

Thoreau used the example of his own act of civil disobedience to illustrate his point. He refused to pay a poll tax that
supported the Mexican-American War and slavery, resulting
in his arrest and imprisonment. Thoreau argued that com-
pliance with unjust laws perpetuates injustice, and it is the
responsibility of conscientious individuals to challenge and
oppose such laws.

Thoreau's ideas on civil disobedience have influenced social
and political movements worldwide, including Mahatma
Gandhi's campaign for Indian independence and Martin
Luther King Jr.'s civil rights movement. His emphasis on
moral integrity and nonviolent resistance continues to inspire activism and the pursuit of social justice.

July 15: Henry David Thoreau - Simple Living

T HOREAU IS ALSO KNOWN for his advocacy of simple living, as articulated in his book "Walden." He believed that living simply and in harmony with nature leads to greater self-awareness, spiritual fulfillment, and freedom from materialistic pursuits. Thoreau's experiment in simple living involved building a small cabin near Walden Pond and living there for two years, focusing on self-sufficiency and reflection.

Thoreau used the example of his daily routine at Walden Pond to illustrate the benefits of simple living. He spent his days engaging in activities like reading, writing, gardening, and observing nature. Thoreau argued that simplifying one's life and reducing dependence on material possessions allows individuals to focus on what truly matters and fosters personal growth.

Thoreau's philosophy of simple living has influenced various movements, including environmentalism, minimalism, and sustainable living. His ideas encourage a reevaluation of modern consumer culture and the pursuit of a more intentional and meaningful life.

July 16: Henry David Thoreau - Harmony with Nature

T HOREAU'S PHILOSOPHY ALSO EMPHASIZES the importance of living in harmony with nature. He believed that nature provides a source of inspiration, wisdom, and spiritual renewal. Thoreau's writings reflect his deep appreciation for the natural world and his belief that a close connection with nature is essential for personal well-being and environmental stewardship.

Thoreau used the example of his observations of the changing seasons at Walden Pond to illustrate the interconnectedness of life. He noted how the cycles of nature mirror the cycles of human existence, offering insights into the rhythms and patterns of life. Thoreau argued that spending time in nature helps individuals cultivate a sense of peace, clarity, and reverence for the environment.

Thoreau's emphasis on harmony with nature has had a lasting impact on environmental philosophy and conservation efforts. His ideas inspire a deeper appreciation for the natural world and advocate for the protection and preservation of the environment.

July 17: Charles Sanders Peirce - Pragmatic Maxim: Meaning of Concepts

C HARLES SANDERS PEIRCE, AN American philosopher and logician, is considered the founder of pragmatism. His pragmatic maxim states that the meaning of a concept lies in its practical effects and implications. According to Peirce, to understand a concept, one must consider how it influences behavior and experience.

Peirce used the example of hardness to illustrate the pragmatic maxim. He argued that the meaning of "hardness" is understood through its practical effects, such as resistance to scratching or deformation. By focusing on the observable consequences of a concept, Peirce's pragmatic approach provides a practical framework for understanding and evaluating ideas.

Peirce's pragmatic maxim has influenced various fields, including philosophy, science, and linguistics. His emphasis on the practical consequences of concepts continues to shape discussions on meaning, truth, and the application of ideas in real-world contexts.

July 18: Charles Sanders Peirce - Fallibilism: The Impermanence of Knowledge

PEIRCE INTRODUCED THE CONCEPT of fallibilism, the idea that all human knowledge is inherently uncertain and subject to revision. He argued that our understanding of the world is always provisional and that scientific inquiry is a continuous process of hypothesis testing and refinement. Fallibilism acknowledges the limitations of human cognition and the potential for error.

Peirce used the example of scientific theories to illustrate fallibilism. He noted that even well-established scientific theories, such as Newtonian mechanics, can be revised or replaced in light of new evidence, as happened with the advent of Einstein's theory of relativity. This iterative process of inquiry reflects the evolving nature of knowledge.

Peirce's fallibilism has influenced contemporary epistemology and the philosophy of science, emphasizing the importance of openness to new evidence and the ongoing quest for understanding. His ideas encourage a humble and adaptive approach to knowledge, recognizing the dynamic and tentative nature of human inquiry.

July 19: Charles Sanders Peirce - Semiotics: Theory of Signs

P EIRCE IS ALSO KNOWN for his contributions to semiotics, the study of signs and symbols. He developed a comprehensive theory of signs, defining a sign as anything that conveys meaning and representing the relationship between the sign, its object, and its interpretant (the interpretation of the sign). Peirce's semiotic theory explores how signs function and how meaning is constructed.

Peirce used the example of a stop sign to illustrate his theory of signs. The stop sign (the sign) represents the concept of stopping (the object), and drivers interpret the sign as a command to stop their vehicles (the interpretant). This triadic relationship forms the basis of Peirce's semiotics and highlights the complexity of meaning-making.

Peirce's semiotic theory has influenced linguistics, communication studies, and cultural analysis, providing a framework for understanding how signs and symbols operate in various contexts. His work underscores the importance of interpretation and the interplay between signs and meaning in human communication.

July 20: William James - Pragmatism: Truth as What Works

W ILLIAM JAMES, AN AMERICAN philosopher and psychologist, further developed the philosophy of pragmatism. James argued that the truth of an idea or belief is determined by its practical consequences and usefulness. According to James, an idea is true if it effectively guides action and helps individuals navigate their experiences.

James used the example of religious beliefs to illustrate pragmatism. He argued that if believing in a higher power provides comfort, motivation, and ethical guidance, then that belief is pragmatically true for the individual. This practical approach to truth emphasizes the functional role of beliefs in shaping human behavior and well-being.

James' pragmatism has influenced various fields, including psychology, education, and philosophy. His emphasis on the practical implications of ideas continues to inform discussions on the nature of truth, belief, and the value of different perspectives.

July 21: William James - The Will to Believe

WILLIAM JAMES IS ALSO known for his essay "The Will to Believe," in which he argues that individuals have the right to hold beliefs based on personal and pragmatic grounds, especially in situations where evidence is inconclusive. James believed that the decision to believe in certain propositions, such as religious faith, often involves a leap of faith driven by personal and practical considerations.

James used the example of friendship to illustrate the will to believe. He argued that forming a friendship often requires trust and a willingness to believe in the goodwill of the other person, even in the absence of conclusive evidence. This act of faith can create meaningful and fulfilling relationships.

James' concept of the will to believe highlights the interplay between reason, emotion, and practical considerations in forming beliefs. His ideas encourage a more flexible and inclusive approach to understanding belief systems, acknowledging the role of personal experience and the practical benefits of faith.

July 22: William James - Stream of Consciousness

W ILLIAM JAMES INTRODUCED THE concept of the "stream of consciousness" to describe the continuous flow of thoughts, feelings, and perceptions in the human mind. He argued that consciousness is not a series of discrete events but an ongoing, fluid process that reflects the dynamic nature of mental life. This idea has had a significant impact on psychology and literature.

James used the example of daydreaming to illustrate the stream of consciousness. He noted how thoughts seamlessly flow from one to another, often without a clear logical structure, reflecting the spontaneous and ever-changing nature of human cognition. This continuous flow of mental activity shapes our experience of reality.

James' concept of the stream of consciousness influenced literary techniques, particularly in the works of writers like Virginia Woolf and James Joyce, who sought to capture the inner workings of the mind in their narratives. His ideas continue to inform psychological theories on the nature of consciousness and the complexity of human thought.

July 23: Friedrich Nietzsche - Will to Power

F RIEDRICH NIETZSCHE, A GERMAN philosopher, introduced the concept of the "Will to Power" as a fundamental driving force in human beings. According to Nietzsche, the Will to Power is the innate drive to assert and
enhance one's power and influence. This drive goes beyond
mere survival, encompassing creativity, ambition, and the
pursuit of excellence.

Nietzsche used the example of artistic creation to illustrate
the Will to Power. He argued that artists are motivated by
a desire to express their individuality and leave a lasting
impact on the world through their work. This creative im-
pulse reflects the broader human drive to assert one's will
and shape reality according to one's vision.

Nietzsche's concept of the Will to Power has influenced
existentialist and postmodern thought, highlighting the dynamic and often conflictual nature of human existence. His
ideas challenge traditional moral and philosophical frameworks, emphasizing the importance of individual strength,
creativity, and self-assertion.

July 24: Friedrich Nietzsche - Eternal Recurrence

NIETZSCHE'S IDEA OF ETERNAL Recurrence posits that all events in the universe repeat infinitely in a cyclical pattern. This concept challenges individuals to consider how they would live their lives if they were destined to relive the same experiences eternally. Nietzsche believed that embracing Eternal Recurrence can lead to a more authentic and meaningful existence.

Nietzsche used the thought experiment of Eternal Recurrence to provoke introspection. He asked individuals to imagine their lives repeating endlessly and to consider whether they would find this prospect joyous or unbearable. This exercise encourages a reevaluation of one's values, choices, and actions, promoting a life of purpose and intentionality.

Nietzsche's concept of Eternal Recurrence has influenced existentialist philosophy, particularly in its focus on the individual's confrontation with meaning and the significance of personal choices. His ideas encourage a profound engagement with life's challenges and the pursuit of a life worth reliving.

July 25: Friedrich Nietzsche - The Übermensch (Overman)

N IETZSCHE INTRODUCED THE CONCEPT of the Übermensch, or Overman, as an ideal figure who transcends conventional morality and embraces a higher state of existence. The Übermensch represents the next stage of human evolution, characterized by self-mastery, creativity, and the ability to define one's own values.

Nietzsche used the example of the artist-philosopher to illustrate the Übermensch. He envisioned the Übermensch as someone who creates their own meaning and purpose in life, free from the constraints of societal norms and religious dogma. This figure embodies Nietzsche's vision of human potential and the pursuit of greatness.

The concept of the Übermensch has had a significant impact on existentialist and modernist thought, inspiring discussions on human potential, individuality, and the creation of meaning. Nietzsche's ideas challenge individuals to strive for self-overcoming and to cultivate their unique strengths and aspirations.

JULY 26: SIGMUND FREUD - THE UNCONSCIOUS MIND

S IGMUND FREUD, AN AUSTRIAN neurologist and the founder of psychoanalysis, introduced the concept of the unconscious mind as a key element of his theory of human behavior. Freud argued that the unconscious mind contains thoughts, memories, and desires that are not accessible to conscious awareness but influence behavior and emotions.

Freud used the example of dreams to illustrate the unconscious mind. He believed that dreams are a window into the unconscious, revealing hidden desires and conflicts through symbolic imagery. By analyzing dreams, Freud sought to uncover the underlying psychological issues affecting an individual's conscious life.

Freud's concept of the unconscious mind has had a profound impact on psychology, psychiatry, and the arts. His ideas have influenced the understanding of human behavior, the development of therapeutic techniques, and the exploration of the depths of the human psyche.

July 27: Sigmund Freud - Psychoanalysis: Exploring Repressed Memories

F REUD DEVELOPED PSYCHOANALYSIS AS a method for exploring and treating psychological disorders by uncovering and addressing repressed memories and emotions. He believed that many psychological issues stem from unresolved conflicts and traumas that are buried in the unconscious mind. Through techniques such as free association, dream analysis, and transference, Freud aimed to bring these repressed elements to conscious awareness.

Freud used the example of a patient with hysteria to illustrate psychoanalysis. He found that by encouraging the patient to speak freely about their thoughts and feelings, repressed memories and emotions would surface, leading to insights and healing. This process of uncovering and working through unconscious material became the cornerstone of psychoanalytic therapy.

Freud's development of psychoanalysis revolutionized the field of mental health, providing a framework for understanding and treating psychological disorders. His methods and theories continue to influence contemporary psychotherapy and the exploration of the human mind.

July 28: Sigmund Freud - Defense Mechanisms: Ways of Coping with Anxiety

F REUD ALSO IDENTIFIED VARIOUS defense mechanisms that individuals use to cope with anxiety and protect themselves from psychological distress. These unconscious strategies help manage internal conflicts and emotional pain but can also distort reality and hinder personal growth. Some common defense mechanisms include repression, denial, projection, and displacement.

Freud used the example of repression to explain defense mechanisms. He argued that individuals often push threatening or painful thoughts and memories out of conscious awareness to avoid emotional discomfort. While repression can provide temporary relief, it can also lead to unresolved conflicts and psychological issues if not addressed.

Freud's exploration of defense mechanisms has influenced the understanding of human behavior and the development of therapeutic techniques. His ideas highlight the complex ways in which individuals cope with stress and anxiety, providing valuable insights for psychological treatment and personal development.

July 29: Henri Bergson - Élan Vital (Vital Force)

H ENRI BERGSON, A FRENCH philosopher, introduced the concept of élan vital, or vital force, to describe the creative and dynamic force that drives the evolution and development of life. Bergson believed that this vital force is a fundamental aspect of living organisms, guiding their growth, adaptation, and complexity in ways that cannot be fully explained by mechanistic or deterministic theories.

Bergson used the example of biological evolution to illustrate élan vital. He argued that the complexity and diversity of life cannot be solely attributed to natural selection and random mutations. Instead, there is a creative force that propels life forward, enabling organisms to develop new forms and functions that transcend purely material explanations.

Bergson's concept of élan vital influenced subsequent philosophical and scientific discussions on the nature of life and creativity. His ideas challenge reductionist approaches, emphasizing the importance of considering the dynamic and holistic aspects of living systems.

JULY 30: HENRI BERGSON - INTUITION AS A METHOD OF UNDERSTANDING

HENRI BERGSON ALSO EMPHASIZED the importance of intuition as a method of understanding reality, contrasting it with analytical and scientific approaches. He believed that intuition allows individuals to grasp the essence of things directly, without breaking them down into parts. Intuition provides a deeper, more immediate insight into the nature of reality, particularly in relation to time and consciousness.

Bergson used the example of experiencing music to illustrate intuition. He argued that while one can analyze a piece of music by examining its notes and structure, the true essence of the music is felt through intuitive appreciation. This direct, holistic experience captures the flow and emotional impact of the music, which analytical methods might miss.

Bergson's advocacy for intuition has influenced existentialist and phenomenological thought, encouraging a more holistic and experiential approach to understanding human consciousness and reality. His ideas highlight the limitations of purely analytical methods and the value of direct, intuitive insight.

July 31: Henri Bergson - Duration: Subjective Experience of Time

B ERGSON'S CONCEPT OF DURATION (la durée) addresses the subjective experience of time, distinguishing it from the objective, measurable time of clocks and calendars. He argued that real time, or duration, is qualitative and continuous, experienced as a flow of consciousness rather than a sequence of discrete moments. This perspective emphasizes the fluidity and complexity of temporal experience.

Bergson used the example of personal memory to illustrate duration. He noted that recalling a past event involves reliving it in a continuous, unfolding manner, where emotions, sensations, and thoughts intermingle. This subjective experience contrasts with the objective measurement of time, which breaks it into uniform units.

Bergson's exploration of duration has had a profound impact on philosophy, psychology, and literature. His ideas challenge conventional notions of time and encourage a deeper appreciation of the subjective, lived experience of temporality.

AUGUST 1: JOHN DEWEY - PRAGMATISM: PRACTICAL APPLICATION OF IDEAS

JOHN DEWEY, AN AMERICAN philosopher and educator, was a leading proponent of pragmatism, a philosophical approach that emphasizes the practical application of ideas. Dewey believed that concepts and theories should be evaluated based on their usefulness and impact on real-world situations. He argued that knowledge is best understood through its effects on experience and action.

Dewey used the example of problem-solving to illustrate pragmatism. He argued that when faced with a practical issue, individuals should test different solutions through experimentation and observation. The most effective solution is one that produces the desired results in a given context, reflecting the pragmatic criterion of truth.

Dewey's pragmatic approach has influenced various fields, including education, psychology, and public policy. His emphasis on practical outcomes and experiential learning continues to shape contemporary thought and practice.

AUGUST 2: JOHN DEWEY - EDUCATION: LEARNING BY DOING

J OHN DEWEY WAS A strong advocate for experiential
education, emphasizing the importance of learning by
doing. He believed that education should be an active and
participatory process, where students engage with their environment and apply their knowledge in practical ways.
Dewey argued that this hands-on approach fosters deeper
understanding and critical thinking skills.

Dewey used the example of science education to illustrate
learning by doing. He suggested that students learn scientific principles more effectively by conducting experiments
and observing results firsthand, rather than merely reading
about them in textbooks. This experiential approach encourages curiosity, problem-solving, and a deeper grasp of
scientific concepts.

Dewey's ideas on education have had a lasting impact on
pedagogical practices, promoting student-centered and in-
quiry-based learning. His emphasis on experiential learning continues to influence educational theories and reforms
worldwide.

AUGUST 3: JOHN DEWEY - DEMOCRACY: IMPORTANCE OF PUBLIC PARTICIPATION

J OHN DEWEY ALSO EMPHASIZED the importance of democracy and public participation in social and political life. He believed that democracy is not just a form of government but a way of living that encourages active engagement, communication, and collaboration among citizens. Dewey argued that democratic participation fosters individual growth and social progress.

Dewey used the example of community involvement to illustrate the importance of public participation. He suggested that individuals should engage in local governance, civic organizations, and public discussions to contribute to the common good and develop their capacities for critical thinking and cooperation.

Dewey's advocacy for democracy has influenced political philosophy and education, emphasizing the role of active citizenship in creating a vibrant and equitable society. His ideas continue to inspire efforts to promote civic engagement and participatory democracy.

August 4: Rabindranath Tagore - Universalism: Embrace of Universal Human Values

R ABINDRANATH TAGORE, AN INDIAN philosopher, poet, and educator, championed the idea of universalism, advocating for the embrace of universal human values that transcend cultural and national boundaries. Tagore believed that all humans share a common spiritual and ethical foundation, which can foster mutual respect, understanding, and harmony among diverse peoples.

Tagore used the example of art and literature to illustrate universalism. He argued that creative expressions, such as poetry and music, resonate with universal human experiences and emotions, enabling people from different backgrounds to connect and empathize with one another. This shared cultural heritage reflects the underlying unity of humanity.

Tagore's universalism has had a significant impact on intercultural dialogue and global education. His ideas encourage the recognition of common human values and the promotion of peace and cooperation across cultures and nations.

AUGUST 5: RABINDRANATH TAGORE - EDUCATION: HOLISTIC AND CREATIVE APPROACHES TO LEARNING

T AGORE WAS A VISIONARY in the field of education, advocating for holistic and creative approaches to learning. He believed that education should nurture the overall development of individuals, including their intellectual, emotional, and spiritual capacities. Tagore's educational philosophy emphasized creativity, critical thinking, and a deep connection with nature.

Tagore used the example of his school, Shantiniketan, to illustrate his educational ideals. At Shantiniketan, students engaged in a variety of activities, such as music, art, literature, and outdoor exploration, fostering a well-rounded and joyful learning experience. Tagore's approach aimed to cultivate free-thinking, creative individuals who could contribute meaningfully to society.

Tagore's educational philosophy has influenced progressive education movements, emphasizing the importance of creativity, experiential learning, and the holistic development of students. His ideas continue to inspire educational reforms that seek to create more nurturing and dynamic learning environments.

August 6: Rabindranath Tagore - Spiritual Humanism: Integration of Spirituality and Humanity

T AGORE'S PHILOSOPHY OF SPIRITUAL humanism integrates spirituality with a deep respect for human dignity and ethical living. He believed that true spirituality is expressed through compassion, service to others, and the pursuit of justice. Tagore argued that spiritual growth and human development are interconnected, and both are essential for a fulfilling life.

Tagore used the example of social service to illustrate spiritual humanism. He believed that helping those in need and working towards social equity are expressions of spiritual values. By serving others, individuals cultivate their own spiritual awareness and contribute to the collective well-being of society.

Tagore's spiritual humanism has had a lasting impact on ethical and spiritual thought, emphasizing the integration of inner spiritual growth with outward social action. His ideas inspire a holistic approach to living that values both personal development and societal contribution.

August 7: Vivekananda - Practical Vedanta: Applying Spiritual Principles in Daily Life

S WAMI VIVEKANANDA, AN INDIAN Hindu monk and
philosopher, emphasized the practical application of
Vedanta, an ancient Indian philosophical system, in daily
life. Vivekananda believed that Vedanta's spiritual principles, such as the unity of all existence and the divinity of the
soul, should guide one's actions, decisions, and interactions
with others.

Vivekananda used the example of selfless service to illustrate Practical Vedanta. He argued that serving others without expecting anything in return is a way to realize the
divine within oneself and others. This practice not only
benefits society but also fosters personal spiritual growth
and fulfillment.

Vivekananda's Practical Vedanta has inspired numerous
social and spiritual movements, encouraging individuals
to integrate spirituality with everyday life. His teachings
continue to influence modern interpretations of Vedanta
and the emphasis on living a spiritually grounded and ser-
vice-oriented life.

August 8: Vivekananda - Universal Religion: Harmony Among Different Faiths

V IVEKANANDA ADVOCATED FOR THE idea of a universal religion that embraces the core truths of all faiths, promoting harmony and understanding among different religious traditions. He believed that all religions share fundamental spiritual principles and that these commonalities should be highlighted to foster unity and peace.

Vivekananda used the example of interfaith dialogue to illustrate the concept of universal religion. He argued that open and respectful discussions among followers of different faiths can reveal shared values and mutual respect, helping to bridge divides and reduce religious conflicts.

Vivekananda's vision of a universal religion has influenced interfaith movements and dialogues worldwide, promoting religious tolerance and cooperation. His ideas encourage the recognition of the universal aspects of spirituality and the celebration of diversity within a framework of mutual respect.

AUGUST 9: VIVEKANANDA - SELF-REALIZATION: ATTAINING TRUE KNOWLEDGE OF ONESELF

V IVEKANANDA EMPHASIZED THE IMPORTANCE of self-realization, the process of attaining true knowledge of oneself and one's divine nature. He believed that self-realization leads to inner peace, strength, and a deeper understanding of one's purpose in life. This spiritual awakening involves transcending the ego and recognizing the interconnectedness of all beings.

Vivekananda used the example of meditation to illustrate the path to self-realization. He argued that through regular meditation and introspection, individuals can quiet the mind, gain insight into their true nature, and experience a profound sense of unity with the universe.

Vivekananda's teachings on self-realization have had a lasting impact on spiritual practices and philosophies around the world. His emphasis on personal spiritual growth and the realization of one's divine potential continues to inspire seekers on the path to enlightenment.

AUGUST 10: MAX WEBER - THE PROTESTANT ETHIC: CONNECTION BETWEEN RELIGION AND CAPITALISM

MAX WEBER, A GERMAN sociologist, is best known for his work "The Protestant Ethic and the Spirit of Capitalism," in which he explores the connection between Protestant ethics, particularly Calvinism, and the development of capitalism. Weber argued that the values of hard work, discipline, and frugality promoted by Protestantism played a significant role in shaping modern capitalist economies.

Weber used the example of the "calling" to illustrate his theory. He believed that the Protestant idea of a calling, where individuals see their work as a divine vocation, encouraged a strong work ethic and the accumulation of wealth as a sign of God's favor. This religious motivation, according to Weber, contributed to the rise of capitalist economies in Protestant regions.

Weber's analysis of the relationship between religion and economic behavior has influenced sociological and economic thought, highlighting the cultural and ethical dimensions of economic development. His ideas continue to inform discussions on the interplay between religion, culture, and economic systems.

August 11: Max Weber - Bureaucracy: Analysis of Organizational Structures

M AX WEBER IS ALSO known for his analysis of bureaucracy, which he saw as a defining characteristic of modern organizations and institutions. Weber described bureaucracy as a rational, efficient, and hierarchical system of administration designed to handle complex tasks through standardized procedures and impersonal rules.

Weber used the example of government agencies to illustrate the features of bureaucracy. He argued that bureaucratic organizations are characterized by clear hierarchies, division of labor, formal rules and procedures, and merit-based promotion. These features ensure efficiency, predictability, and accountability in large-scale operations.

Weber's study of bureaucracy has had a profound impact on organizational theory and public administration. His insights into the strengths and limitations of bureaucratic systems continue to influence the design and management of organizations in both the public and private sectors.

August 12: Max Weber - Verstehen: Understanding Human Behavior from the Actor's Perspective

W EBER INTRODUCED THE CONCEPT of Verstehen, a German term meaning "understanding," to emphasize the importance of interpreting human behavior from the perspective of the individuals involved. Verstehen involves empathetic and interpretive analysis, seeking to understand the meanings and motivations behind people's actions within their social and cultural context.

Weber used the example of religious rituals to illustrate Verstehen. He argued that to understand the significance of a religious practice, one must grasp the beliefs, values, and intentions of the participants. This interpretive approach provides deeper insights into social phenomena by considering the subjective experiences of individuals.

Weber's concept of Verstehen has influenced qualitative research methods and interpretive sociology, emphasizing the importance of empathy and context in understanding human behavior. His ideas encourage a more nuanced and comprehensive approach to social analysis.

August 13: Kitaro Nishida - Pure Experience: Immediate Experience as the Basis of Reality

K ITARO NISHIDA, A JAPANESE philosopher, introduced the concept of pure experience as the foundational aspect of reality. According to Nishida, pure experience refers to the direct and immediate experience of reality before it is conceptualized or interpreted by the mind. This state of pure experience reveals the true nature of existence, free from dualistic distinctions.

Nishida used the example of a newborn's perception to illustrate pure experience. He argued that a newborn experiences the world directly, without the cognitive filters and conceptual categories that adults use. This unmediated experience reflects the purest form of encountering reality, where subject and object are not yet separated.

Nishida's concept of pure experience has influenced Japanese philosophy and Zen Buddhism, emphasizing the importance of direct, unmediated awareness. His ideas challenge the dominance of intellectual abstraction and encourage a more holistic and immediate engagement with reality.

August 14: Kitaro Nishida - Basho: Absolute Nothingness as a Fundamental Principle

K ITARO NISHIDA ALSO EXPLORED the concept of basho, or absolute nothingness, as a fundamental principle in his philosophy. Nishida believed that absolute nothingness is the ground of all being and the source of creativity and transformation. This concept is influenced by Zen Buddhism and the idea of emptiness (śūnyatā) as the ultimate reality.

Nishida used the example of artistic creation to illustrate basho. He argued that true creativity arises from a state of absolute nothingness, where the artist transcends personal ego and conceptual limitations. In this state, the artist can access the boundless potential of pure creativity and bring forth original and transformative works.

Nishida's concept of basho has had a significant impact on modern Japanese philosophy and aesthetics. His ideas emphasize the transformative power of embracing emptiness and the potential for profound creativity and insight that arises from this fundamental principle.

AUGUST 15: KITARO NISHIDA - ZEN PHILOSOPHY: INTEGRATION OF ZEN INTO PHILOSOPHICAL INQUIRY

NISHIDA'S PHILOSOPHY IS DEEPLY influenced by Zen Buddhism, and he sought to integrate Zen principles into philosophical inquiry. He believed that Zen's emphasis on direct experience, non-duality, and mindfulness provides valuable insights into the nature of reality and human existence. Nishida's work bridges Eastern and Western philosophical traditions, creating a unique and holistic perspective.

Nishida used the example of Zen meditation (zazen) to illustrate the integration of Zen into philosophy. He argued that the practice of sitting in meditation, focusing on the present moment, and letting go of dualistic thinking leads to a deeper understanding of reality. This experiential approach complements traditional philosophical methods, offering a more immediate and transformative path to knowledge.

Nishida's integration of Zen philosophy has influenced contemporary thought, encouraging a dialogue between Eastern and Western traditions. His ideas highlight the importance of direct experience and mindfulness in philosophical inquiry, fostering a more holistic and inclusive approach to understanding reality.

August 16: D.T. Suzuki - Zen Buddhism: Emphasis on Direct Experience

D.T. SUZUKI, A JAPANESE philosopher and scholar, played a pivotal role in introducing Zen Buddhism to the Western world. Suzuki emphasized the importance of direct experience in Zen practice, advocating for a non-conceptual and immediate engagement with reality. Zen Buddhism, as presented by Suzuki, focuses on experiencing the present moment without the interference of intellectual analysis or dualistic thinking.

Suzuki used the example of zazen, or seated meditation, to illustrate the emphasis on direct experience. In zazen, practitioners sit in silence, focusing on their breath and observing their thoughts without attachment. This practice encourages a direct encounter with one's inner self and the nature of existence, fostering a profound sense of presence and awareness.

Suzuki's teachings on Zen Buddhism have had a significant impact on Western thought, influencing various fields including psychology, philosophy, and the arts. His emphasis on direct experience challenges the predominance of rational, analytical approaches, offering a path to deeper self-understanding and spiritual insight.

August 17: D.T. Suzuki - Satori: Sudden Enlightenment

D.T. SUZUKI ALSO INTRODUCED Western audiences to the concept of satori, or sudden enlightenment, a key element of Zen Buddhism. Satori represents a profound and transformative realization of one's true nature and the nature of reality. This experience often occurs spontaneously, breaking through the ordinary confines of thought and perception.

Suzuki used the example of a Zen koan, a paradoxical question or statement used in meditation practice, to illustrate the process leading to satori. By contemplating a koan, such as "What is the sound of one hand clapping?", practitioners engage in intense introspection, eventually breaking through intellectual barriers to experience a moment of sudden clarity and insight.

The concept of satori has fascinated Western thinkers and practitioners, highlighting the potential for instantaneous spiritual awakening. Suzuki's explanation of satori underscores the transformative power of Zen practice and its emphasis on direct, experiential knowledge.

August 18: D.T. Suzuki - Meditation: Practice as a Path to Insight

S UZUKI EMPHASIZED MEDITATION AS a core practice in Zen Buddhism, essential for achieving insight and spiritual growth. Meditation, particularly zazen, is viewed as a discipline that quiets the mind, allowing practitioners to observe their thoughts and emotions without attachment. Through regular meditation, individuals can develop greater self-awareness and a deeper understanding of their true nature.

Suzuki used the example of mindfulness in everyday activities to illustrate the application of meditation. He suggested that by practicing mindfulness while performing simple tasks, such as eating or walking, individuals can cultivate a state of continuous awareness and presence. This practice helps integrate the insights gained from meditation into daily life, fostering a more harmonious and centered existence.

Suzuki's teachings on meditation have had a lasting influence on both Eastern and Western spiritual practices. His emphasis on the practical benefits of meditation highlights its role in personal development and the pursuit of enlightenment.

AUGUST 19: BERTRAND RUSSELL - LOGICAL ANALYSIS

B ERTRAND RUSSELL, A BRITISH philosopher and logician, is renowned for his contributions to logical analysis. Russell believed that philosophical problems could be clarified and resolved through precise logical reasoning and the analysis of language. His work in this area laid the foundation for much of modern analytic philosophy, emphasizing the importance of clarity and rigor in philosophical inquiry.

Russell used the example of logical positivism to illustrate logical analysis. He argued that meaningful statements are those that can be empirically verified or logically proven, dismissing metaphysical and theological claims as nonsensical. This approach sought to bring the precision of mathematical logic to the study of philosophy, aiming for clear and unambiguous arguments.

Russell's emphasis on logical analysis has profoundly impacted the field of philosophy, promoting a scientific and analytical approach to philosophical questions. His ideas continue to influence contemporary philosophical discourse and the development of formal logic.

AUGUST 20: BERTRAND RUSSELL - ANTI-IDEALISM: REJECTION OF HEGELIAN METAPHYSICS

R USSELL WAS A STAUNCH critic of idealism, partic-ularly the metaphysical theories of G.W.F. Hegel. He rejected the idea that reality is fundamentally mental or spiritual, instead advocating for a form of realism that rec-ognizes the existence of an external, objective world. Rus-sell's anti-idealism was part of his broader effort to ground philosophy in empirical science and logical analysis.

Russell used the example of sense perception to argue against idealism. He maintained that our sensory experi-ences provide direct evidence of an external reality, inde-pendent of our minds. This stance opposed the idealist view that reality is a construct of the mind, asserting instead that the physical world exists regardless of our perception of it.

Russell's rejection of idealism influenced the development of analytic philosophy and the emphasis on empirical and scientific methods. His work encouraged a shift away from speculative metaphysics towards a more practical and evi-dence-based approach to philosophical problems.

AUGUST 21: BERTRAND RUSSELL - ANALYTIC PHILOSOPHY: FOCUS ON LANGUAGE AND LOGIC

R USSELL IS ALSO A key figure in the development of analytic philosophy, which focuses on the analysis of language and logic to clarify philosophical issues. He believed that many philosophical problems arise from misunderstandings or misuses of language and that careful analysis can dissolve these problems by revealing their logical structure.

Russell used the example of definite descriptions to illustrate analytic philosophy. In his theory of descriptions, he analyzed sentences containing phrases like "the current King of France" to show how language can mislead us into thinking there are real entities corresponding to these phrases. By dissecting the logical form of such sentences, Russell demonstrated how philosophical clarity can be achieved.

Russell's focus on language and logic has had a profound impact on the field of philosophy, influencing the work of later philosophers such as Ludwig Wittgenstein and the logical positivists. His approach continues to shape contemporary philosophical practice, emphasizing the importance of linguistic precision and logical rigor.

August 22: Sri Aurobindo - Integral Yoga: Integration of Spiritual and Material Life

S RI AUROBINDO, AN INDIAN philosopher and spiritual leader, developed the concept of Integral Yoga, which seeks to integrate spiritual and material aspects of life. Aurobindo believed that true spiritual growth involves harmonizing the inner and outer dimensions of existence, fostering a balanced and holistic approach to self-realization.

Aurobindo used the example of daily work to illustrate Integral Yoga. He argued that engaging in everyday activities with mindfulness and dedication transforms them into spiritual practices. By seeing work as an offering to the divine, individuals can cultivate inner growth while contributing to the world around them, achieving a synthesis of spiritual and material pursuits.

Aurobindo's Integral Yoga has influenced contemporary spiritual practices and holistic approaches to personal development. His ideas encourage a comprehensive approach to spirituality, emphasizing the integration of all aspects of life.

August 23: Sri Aurobindo - Supermind: Higher Level of Consciousness

S RI AUROBINDO INTRODUCED THE concept of the Supermind, a higher level of consciousness that transcends the limitations of ordinary human thinking. According to Aurobindo, the Supermind represents a state of divine consciousness, where individuals can access a deeper, intuitive understanding of reality and experience unity with the divine.

Aurobindo used the example of intuition to illustrate the Supermind. He believed that while ordinary thinking relies on rational analysis and sensory perception, the Supermind operates through direct, intuitive knowledge. This higher consciousness enables individuals to perceive the interconnectedness of all things and to act with greater wisdom and insight.

Aurobindo's concept of the Supermind has influenced spiritual and philosophical thought, highlighting the potential for human consciousness to evolve and access higher states of awareness. His ideas continue to inspire seekers on the path to spiritual enlightenment and self-realization.

AUGUST 24: SRI AUROBINDO - EVOLUTION: SPIRITUAL EVOLUTION OF HUMANITY

A UROBINDO'S PHILOSOPHY ALSO EMPHASIZES the idea of spiritual evolution, proposing that humanity is on a path towards higher consciousness and spiritual development. He believed that human evolution is not merely a biological process but also a spiritual journey, where individuals and societies gradually realize their divine potential.

Aurobindo used the example of societal progress to illustrate spiritual evolution. He argued that advancements in culture, science, and ethics reflect humanity's ongoing spiritual development. As individuals awaken to their higher consciousness, they contribute to the collective evolution of society, fostering greater harmony, creativity, and enlightenment.

Aurobindo's vision of spiritual evolution has had a lasting impact on philosophical and spiritual discourse. His ideas encourage a broader perspective on human development, recognizing the interconnectedness of individual growth and collective progress.

August 25: Carl Gustav Jung - Collective Unconscious

C ARL GUSTAV JUNG, A Swiss psychiatrist and psychoanalyst, introduced the concept of the collective unconscious, a part of the unconscious mind that contains shared memories, instincts, and archetypes common to all humans. Unlike Freud's personal unconscious, which is unique to the individual, the collective unconscious is inherited and universal, influencing behavior and experiences across cultures.

Jung used the example of archetypes to illustrate the collective unconscious. Archetypes are recurring symbols and themes, such as the Hero, the Mother, and the Shadow, that appear in myths, dreams, and cultural narratives worldwide. These archetypes reflect fundamental human experiences and provide a framework for understanding the deeper layers of the psyche.

Jung's concept of the collective unconscious has had a significant impact on psychology, anthropology, and cultural studies. His ideas offer a deeper understanding of the universal aspects of human experience and the underlying patterns that shape our thoughts and behaviors.

August 26: Carl Gustav Jung - Individuation

J UNG ALSO INTRODUCED THE process of individuation, a journey towards self-realization and the integration of the conscious and unconscious aspects of the psyche. Individuation involves recognizing and harmonizing the various parts of the self, including the persona, shadow, anima/animus, and the Self, to achieve psychological wholeness.

Jung used the example of the Hero's journey to illustrate individuation. He saw the Hero's journey, a common motif in myths and stories, as a symbolic representation of the individuation process. The Hero faces challenges, encounters inner conflicts, and ultimately achieves a deeper understanding of themselves and their place in the world.

Jung's concept of individuation has influenced therapeutic practices and personal development, encouraging individuals to explore and integrate their unconscious aspects. His ideas highlight the importance of self-awareness and inner harmony in achieving psychological health and fulfillment.

AUGUST 27: CARL GUSTAV JUNG - ARCHETYPES

J UNG'S THEORY OF ARCHETYPES is a central element
of his analytical psychology. Archetypes are innate, universal symbols and motifs that shape human experience
and behavior. They reside in the collective unconscious and
manifest in dreams, myths, and cultural narratives, providing a framework for understanding the deeper aspects of the
human psyche.

Jung used the example of the Shadow archetype to illustrate his theory. The Shadow represents the darker, hidden
aspects of the personality that are often repressed or denied. Confronting and integrating the Shadow is essential
for personal growth and self-awareness, as it brings unconscious elements into conscious awareness.

Jung's exploration of archetypes has influenced various
fields, including psychology, literature, and art. His ideas
provide valuable insights into the universal patterns that
underlie human behavior and the ways in which these patterns are expressed across different cultures and contexts.

AUGUST 28: SAID NURSI - FAITH AND REASON: HARMONY BETWEEN RELIGIOUS BELIEF AND RATIONAL THOUGHT

SAID NURSI, A TURKISH Islamic scholar, emphasized the harmony between faith and reason, arguing that religious belief and rational thought are not mutually exclusive but complementary. Nursi believed that faith should be based on rational understanding and that reason should be guided by spiritual insights. This integration fosters a deeper and more holistic approach to knowledge and spirituality.

Nursi used the example of the natural world to illustrate the harmony between faith and reason. He argued that the complexity and order of the universe provide evidence of a divine creator, and that scientific inquiry can enhance one's appreciation of divine wisdom. By studying nature, individuals can strengthen their faith and gain a deeper understanding of God's creation.

Nursi's emphasis on the integration of faith and reason has influenced contemporary Islamic thought, encouraging a balanced approach to religious belief and intellectual inquiry. His ideas promote the development of a more enlightened and rational spirituality.

August 29: Said Nursi - Modernity: Islam's Response to Modern Challenges

N URSI ADDRESSED THE CHALLENGES posed by modernity to Islamic thought and practice, advocating for a response that embraces positive aspects of modernity while remaining faithful to Islamic principles. He believed that Muslims should engage with modern science, technology, and education, using these tools to enhance their understanding of the world and their faith.

Nursi used the example of education reform to illustrate Islam's response to modernity. He argued that Islamic education should incorporate modern scientific knowledge alongside traditional religious teachings. This integrated approach equips individuals with the skills and understanding needed to navigate the complexities of the modern world while remaining grounded in their faith.

Nursi's ideas on modernity have influenced Islamic reform movements, promoting a dynamic and adaptive approach to contemporary challenges. His vision encourages Muslims to embrace progress and innovation while upholding their spiritual and ethical values.

August 30: Said Nursi - Education: Importance of Knowledge and Learning in Islam

NURSI PLACED A STRONG emphasis on the importance of knowledge and learning in Islam, advocating for a comprehensive and holistic approach to education. He believed that both religious and secular knowledge are essential for personal and societal development, and that education should foster intellectual, moral, and spiritual growth.

Nursi used the example of the Quran to highlight the significance of knowledge in Islam. He argued that the Quran encourages the pursuit of knowledge and understanding, urging believers to reflect on the signs of God in the natural world and to seek wisdom. By integrating religious and secular education, individuals can develop a balanced and enlightened perspective.

Nursi's emphasis on education has had a lasting impact on Islamic thought and practice, promoting the value of lifelong learning and intellectual engagement. His ideas continue to inspire efforts to improve educational systems and to foster a more knowledgeable and informed Muslim community.

AUGUST 31: José Ortega y Gasset - Mass Society

J OSÉ ORTEGA Y GASSET, a Spanish philosopher, is known for his critique of mass society and the effects of modernity on individual autonomy and cultural development. Ortega y Gasset argued that the rise of mass society leads to the dominance of mediocrity and the suppression of individuality, as people conform to standardized norms and behaviors.

Ortega y Gasset used the example of mass media to illustrate his critique. He believed that mass media promotes superficiality and conformity, shaping public opinion and culture in ways that discourage critical thinking and individuality. The influence of mass media contributes to the homogenization of society, undermining the richness of diverse perspectives and creative expression.

Ortega y Gasset's critique of mass society has influenced contemporary discussions on culture, media, and social dynamics. His ideas highlight the importance of preserving individual autonomy and promoting cultural diversity in the face of mass conformity.

September 1: José Ortega y Gasset - Historical Reason

O RTEGA Y GASSET INTRODUCED the concept of historical reason, emphasizing the importance of understanding human existence within its historical context. He argued that individuals and societies are shaped by their historical circumstances, and that reason must be applied to interpret the past and its influence on the present.

Ortega y Gasset used the example of cultural traditions to illustrate historical reason. He believed that cultural practices and beliefs are products of historical development, reflecting the experiences and values of past generations. By studying history, individuals can gain insights into the roots of contemporary issues and develop a deeper appreciation of their cultural heritage.

Ortega y Gasset's concept of historical reason has influenced historiography and cultural studies, encouraging a nuanced and context-sensitive approach to understanding human behavior and social phenomena. His ideas underscore the interconnectedness of past and present, and the importance of historical awareness in shaping a more informed and reflective society.

September 2: José Ortega y Gasset - Vital Reason

O RTEGA Y GASSET ALSO developed the concept of vital reason, which integrates rational thought with the lived experiences and practical concerns of individuals. He believed that philosophy should address the concrete realities of human life, taking into account the dynamic and evolving nature of existence.

Ortega y Gasset used the example of personal decision-making to illustrate vital reason. He argued that rational choices must consider the unique circumstances and context of each individual, rather than relying solely on abstract principles. Vital reason emphasizes the importance of adaptability and responsiveness to the changing conditions of life.

Ortega y Gasset's concept of vital reason has influenced existentialist and phenomenological thought, promoting a more holistic and practical approach to philosophy. His ideas encourage a philosophy that is grounded in the realities of human experience and responsive to the complexities of life.

September 3: Ludwig Wittgenstein - Picture Theory of Language

L UDWIG WITTGENSTEIN, AN AUSTRIAN-BRITISH philosopher, made significant contributions to the philosophy of language. His early work, especially in "Tractatus Logico-Philosophicus," introduced the Picture Theory of Language. Wittgenstein proposed that language functions as a picture of reality, with sentences representing states of affairs by mirroring their logical structure.

Wittgenstein used the example of a blueprint to illustrate his theory. Just as a blueprint represents the structure of a building, a sentence represents the structure of a situation in the world. This correspondence between language and reality allows us to communicate meaningfully about the world.

Wittgenstein's Picture Theory of Language influenced the logical positivists and the development of analytic philosophy. His ideas emphasize the importance of understanding the logical form of language to clarify philosophical problems and our representation of the world.

September 4: Ludwig Wittgenstein - Language Games: Meaning through Use

I N HIS LATER WORK, particularly in "Philosophical Investigations," Wittgenstein shifted his focus to the concept of language games. He argued that the meaning of words is determined by their use in specific social contexts, rather than by their correspondence to objects or states of affairs. Language games are the various ways in which language is used in different activities and forms of life.

Wittgenstein used the example of teaching a child to count to illustrate language games. He noted that the meaning of numbers and counting emerges from the practice of counting objects, not from any inherent connection between numbers and objects. This practical approach highlights how language acquires meaning through its role in human activities.

Wittgenstein's concept of language games has had a profound impact on the philosophy of language and linguistic theory. His ideas emphasize the social and contextual nature of meaning, challenging more rigid, formalistic approaches to understanding language.

September 5: Ludwig Wittgenstein - Limits of Language: What Cannot Be Spoken

W ITTGENSTEIN ALSO EXPLORED THE limits of language, famously concluding in "Tractatus Logico-Philosophicus" that "Whereof one cannot speak, thereof one must be silent." He believed that language can only meaningfully discuss what can be clearly represented and logically structured. Mystical, ethical, and metaphysical matters lie beyond the realm of language and cannot be adequately expressed in words.

Wittgenstein used the example of the mystical experience to illustrate the limits of language. He argued that while one can experience the mystical, it cannot be captured or communicated through language. This boundary reflects the idea that some aspects of human experience are ineffable and must be acknowledged as such.

Wittgenstein's reflections on the limits of language have influenced various philosophical discussions, particularly in areas concerning ethics, religion, and metaphysics. His ideas challenge us to recognize the boundaries of our linguistic and conceptual frameworks and to appreciate the significance of what lies beyond them.

September 6: Martin Heidegger - Being and Time: Inquiry into the Nature of Being

MARTIN HEIDEGGER, A GERMAN philosopher, is renowned for his seminal work "Being and Time," where he delves into the fundamental nature of being. Heidegger argued that traditional philosophy had overlooked the question of what it means to be, focusing instead on specific entities and their properties. He sought to revive this inquiry by exploring the concept of "Being" itself.

Heidegger used the example of a hammer to illustrate his approach. In everyday use, a hammer's "being" is not as an object with specific properties but as something ready-to-hand, integrated into the activity of hammering. When the hammer breaks, its "being" becomes conspicuous as a mere object present-at-hand. This shift highlights the difference between practical engagement and detached contemplation.

Heidegger's exploration of being has influenced existentialism, phenomenology, and postmodern thought. His ideas challenge us to consider our existence and the world in more fundamental terms, beyond conventional philosophical categories.

September 7: Martin Heidegger - Dasein: Human Existence as Being-in-the-World

H EIDEGGER INTRODUCED THE CONCEPT of Dasein, a German term meaning "being there," to describe human existence. Dasein emphasizes that human beings are fundamentally situated in the world, characterized by their relationships, activities, and engagements. This concept rejects the notion of an isolated, abstract self, focusing instead on the holistic experience of being-in-the-world.

Heidegger used the example of a person's relationship with their environment to illustrate Dasein. He argued that our understanding of ourselves and the world arises from our active participation in it, not from detached observation. This perspective highlights the interconnectedness of our being with the world around us.

Heidegger's concept of Dasein has profoundly impacted existential and phenomenological philosophy, encouraging a more integrated and situated understanding of human existence. His ideas emphasize the importance of context, engagement, and the lived experience of being.

September 8: Martin Heidegger - Authenticity: Living True to One's Own Potential

H EIDEGGER ALSO EXPLORED THE idea of authenticity, which involves living true to one's own potential and understanding of being. Authenticity requires confronting the realities of existence, including anxiety and mortality, and making choices that reflect one's true self rather than conforming to societal expectations.

Heidegger used the example of facing one's mortality to illustrate authenticity. He argued that by acknowledging the inevitability of death, individuals can break free from superficial concerns and live more genuinely. This confrontation with mortality encourages a deeper engagement with one's own values and aspirations.

Heidegger's notion of authenticity has influenced existentialist thought, particularly in its focus on personal freedom and self-realization. His ideas challenge individuals to live more consciously and deliberately, embracing their potential and the realities of existence.

September 9: B.R. Ambedkar - Social Justice: Advocacy for Dalit Rights and Equality

B.R. AMBEDKAR, AN INDIAN jurist, economist, and social reformer, is renowned for his advocacy for the rights and equality of Dalits, historically marginalized communities in India. Ambedkar fought against the caste system and worked to promote social justice, believing that true equality could only be achieved through the eradication of caste-based discrimination.

Ambedkar used the example of his own experiences with caste discrimination to highlight the pervasive and damaging effects of the caste system. He argued that legal and social reforms were necessary to dismantle these entrenched inequalities and to provide Dalits with equal opportunities in education, employment, and society.

Ambedkar's advocacy for social justice has had a profound impact on Indian society and the global human rights movement. His work continues to inspire efforts to combat discrimination and to promote equality and justice for all marginalized communities.

September 10: B.R. Ambedkar - Constitutionalism: Rule of Law and Democracy in India

A MBEDKAR PLAYED A CRUCIAL role in the drafting of the Indian Constitution, emphasizing the principles of constitutionalism, rule of law, and democracy. He believed that a strong constitutional framework was essential for protecting individual rights, ensuring social justice, and promoting democratic governance.

Ambedkar used the example of the fundamental rights enshrined in the Indian Constitution to illustrate his commitment to constitutionalism. He ensured that the Constitution guaranteed equal protection under the law, freedom of speech and religion, and protection against discrimination. These provisions aimed to create a just and equitable society where all citizens could enjoy their rights and freedoms.

Ambedkar's contributions to constitutionalism have shaped the legal and political landscape of India. His vision for a democratic and inclusive society continues to guide efforts to uphold the rule of law and to protect the rights of all citizens.

SEPTEMBER 11: B.R. AMBEDKAR - ANNIHILATION OF CASTE: CRITIQUE OF CASTE SYSTEM

AMBEDKAR'S SEMINAL WORK, "ANNIHILATION of Caste," is a powerful critique of the caste system and a call for its complete eradication. He argued that the caste system perpetuates social and economic inequalities and that true social reform requires the abolition of caste-based discrimination and hierarchy.

Ambedkar used the example of inter-caste marriage to illustrate a practical approach to annihilating caste. He believed that encouraging inter-caste marriages would help break down social barriers and promote social integration. This, along with legal and educational reforms, would contribute to dismantling the caste system and fostering a more egalitarian society.

Ambedkar's critique of the caste system remains a cornerstone of social justice movements in India and beyond. His ideas continue to inspire efforts to challenge and eradicate caste-based discrimination, promoting a more just and inclusive society.

September 12: Mikhail Bakhtin - Dialogism: Interaction of Multiple Voices in Texts

MIKHAIL BAKHTIN, A RUSSIAN philosopher and literary critic, introduced the concept of dialogism, emphasizing the interaction of multiple voices and perspectives within texts. He argued that meaning is not produced in isolation but through the dynamic interplay of different voices, reflecting the social and relational nature of language.

Bakhtin used the example of the novel to illustrate dialogism. In novels, characters' voices interact with each other and with the author's voice, creating a rich tapestry of perspectives and meanings. This dialogic process allows for a deeper exploration of themes and the complexity of human experience.

Bakhtin's concept of dialogism has influenced literary theory, linguistics, and cultural studies, highlighting the importance of diversity and interaction in the creation of meaning. His ideas encourage a more nuanced and multi-voiced approach to understanding texts and communication.

September 13: Mikhail Bakhtin - Carnival: Subversion of Social Norms through Festivity

B AKHTIN ALSO EXPLORED THE concept of carnival, viewing it as a social phenomenon where traditional hierarchies and norms are temporarily subverted through festivity and humor. Carnival, according to Bakhtin, represents a space where societal rules are suspended, allowing for the expression of alternative perspectives and the celebration of human creativity and freedom.

Bakhtin used the example of medieval carnival celebrations to illustrate this concept. During these events, the rigid social order was inverted, with peasants becoming kings and vice versa, creating a space for free expression and critical reflection on societal structures. This temporary subversion provided a release from the constraints of everyday life and an opportunity for renewal.

Bakhtin's concept of carnival has influenced cultural studies and critical theory, highlighting the potential for social transformation through festivity and humor. His ideas encourage a recognition of the liberating and transformative power of subversive cultural practices.

September 14: Mikhail Bakhtin - Heteroglossia: Diversity of Voices within a Language

B AKHTIN'S THEORY OF HETEROGLOSSIA emphasizes the diversity of voices and expressions within a language. He argued that language is inherently heterogeneous, composed of multiple social dialects, professional jargons, and individual expressions. This diversity reflects the complex social fabric and the multiplicity of perspectives within any given society.

Bakhtin used the example of a city to illustrate heteroglossia. In a city, various social groups, professions, and individuals coexist, each with their distinct ways of speaking and understanding the world. This linguistic diversity creates a rich and dynamic environment where different voices interact and influence each other.

Bakhtin's concept of heteroglossia has had a significant impact on literary theory and sociolinguistics, emphasizing the importance of recognizing and valuing linguistic diversity. His ideas challenge monolithic views of language and promote a more inclusive and multifaceted understanding of communication.

September 15: Herbert Marcuse - One-Dimensional Man: Critique of Advanced Industrial Society

H ERBERT MARCUSE, A GERMAN-AMERICAN philosopher and sociologist, is known for his critical analysis of advanced industrial society, particularly in his work
"One-Dimensional Man." Marcuse argued that modern capitalist societies create one-dimensional individuals who
conform to established norms and consumerist values, losing their critical and creative capacities.

Marcuse used the example of mass media and advertising
to illustrate his critique. He argued that these institutions
promote a superficial and homogeneous culture, shaping
desires and behaviors to fit the needs of the capitalist system. This process suppresses critical thinking and genuine
individuality, creating a society of passive consumers.

Marcuse's critique of advanced industrial society has influenced critical theory and social philosophy, encouraging a deeper examination of the ways in which economic
and social structures shape human consciousness. His ideas
continue to inspire efforts to promote critical awareness and
social change.

September 16: Herbert Marcuse - Repressive Tolerance: Limits of Liberal Tolerance

M ARCUSE INTRODUCED THE CONCEPT of repressive tolerance, arguing that in a capitalist society, tolerance can become a tool of oppression. He believed that allowing all ideas and behaviors, including those that reinforce the status quo and inequality, ultimately perpetuates existing power structures and inhibits genuine social progress.

Marcuse used the example of political discourse to illustrate repressive tolerance. He argued that in a society where harmful ideologies, such as racism and fascism, are tolerated under the guise of free speech, true freedom and equality are undermined. This false tolerance serves to protect the interests of the powerful and suppress meaningful dissent.

Marcuse's concept of repressive tolerance has sparked debates on the nature of freedom, tolerance, and the conditions necessary for genuine democracy. His ideas challenge us to reconsider the boundaries of tolerance and the role of critical thinking in achieving social justice.

SEPTEMBER 17: HERBERT MARCUSE - CRITICAL THEORY: EMPHASIS ON SOCIAL CHANGE

MARCUSE WAS A LEADING figure in the Frankfurt School of Critical Theory, which emphasizes the importance of social critique and the pursuit of social change. Critical Theory seeks to uncover the underlying power dynamics and ideologies that shape society, aiming to promote human emancipation and a more just and equitable world.

Marcuse used the example of education to illustrate the goals of Critical Theory. He argued that education should not merely transmit knowledge but also foster critical thinking and awareness of social injustices. By empowering individuals to question and challenge the status quo, education can become a tool for social transformation.

Marcuse's emphasis on social change has influenced various fields, including sociology, political science, and cultural studies. His ideas encourage a critical examination of society and the active pursuit of justice and equality.

SEPTEMBER 18: GILBERT RYLE - THE CONCEPT OF MIND: CRITIQUE OF CARTESIAN DUALISM

G ILBERT RYLE, A BRITISH philosopher, is best known for his critique of Cartesian dualism in his work "The Concept of Mind." Ryle argued against René Descartes' idea that the mind and body are separate substances, introducing the concept of the "category mistake" to explain the flawed reasoning behind dualism.

Ryle used the example of a university to illustrate a category mistake. If someone is shown various buildings and departments of a university and then asks, "But where is the university itself?" they are making a category mistake by treating the university as an entity separate from its parts. Similarly, Ryle argued, treating the mind as a distinct entity from the body is a misunderstanding of how mental processes work.

Ryle's critique of Cartesian dualism has influenced the philosophy of mind, promoting a more integrated understanding of mental and physical processes. His ideas challenge the separation of mind and body, emphasizing the importance of considering mental activities in the context of physical behaviors.

September 19: Gilbert Ryle - Category Mistake: Misleading Classifications

RYLE'S CONCEPT OF THE category mistake addresses the errors that arise when concepts or objects are misclassified. He argued that philosophical problems often result from such mistakes, where categories are conflated or concepts are misunderstood as belonging to the wrong logical type.

Ryle used the example of a chess game to illustrate a category mistake. If someone asks, "What is the purpose of the knight piece?" in isolation from the rules and objectives of the game, they are making a category mistake. Understanding the role of the knight requires considering the game as a whole. Similarly, philosophical confusion often arises from misclassifying concepts or ignoring their broader context.

Ryle's concept of the category mistake has had a significant impact on analytic philosophy, encouraging a more precise and context-sensitive approach to philosophical analysis. His ideas highlight the importance of logical clarity and the proper classification of concepts.

September 20: Gilbert Ryle - Dispositional Analysis: Mental States as Tendencies to Behave in Certain Ways

RYLE PROPOSED A DISPOSITIONAL analysis of mental states, arguing that mental states should be understood as tendencies or dispositions to behave in certain ways, rather than as inner, private experiences. This approach contrasts with the Cartesian view of the mind as a repository of conscious thoughts and feelings.

Ryle used the example of believing to illustrate dispositional analysis. He argued that to say someone believes it will rain is to say that they are disposed to carry an umbrella, check the weather forecast, and so on. This dispositional view focuses on observable behaviors and the conditions under which they occur, rather than on inaccessible mental states.

Ryle's dispositional analysis has influenced behaviorism and the philosophy of mind, promoting a more pragmatic and behavior-oriented approach to understanding mental processes. His ideas encourage the examination of how mental states manifest in actions and interactions, rather than treating them as isolated, inner phenomena.

September 21: Nishitani Keiji - Religion and Nothingness: Integration of Zen and Existentialism

NISHITANI KEIJI, A JAPANESE philosopher, is known for his work "Religion and Nothingness," where he integrates Zen Buddhism with existentialist thought. Nishitani explored how the concept of nothingness in Zen Buddhism intersects with existentialist concerns about meaning, existence, and the human condition. He believed that understanding and embracing nothingness could lead to profound spiritual awakening and liberation.

Nishitani used the example of existential anxiety to illustrate his integration of Zen and existentialism. He argued that feelings of meaninglessness and anxiety, central to existentialist thought, can be addressed by the Zen concept of emptiness. By recognizing the inherent emptiness of all things, individuals can transcend their anxieties and find a deeper sense of peace and purpose.

Nishitani's integration of Zen and existentialism has influenced both Eastern and Western philosophical thought, encouraging a dialogue between different traditions. His ideas offer a unique approach to addressing the fundamental questions of human existence and the search for meaning.

September 22: Nishitani Keiji - Emptiness: Central Concept in Zen

A CENTRAL CONCEPT IN Nishitani's philosophy is emptiness (śūnyatā), a key idea in Zen Buddhism. Emptiness refers to the absence of inherent, independent existence in all things, highlighting the interdependent and transient nature of reality. Nishitani believed that realizing emptiness is essential for spiritual liberation and enlightenment.

Nishitani used the example of a flower to explain emptiness. He pointed out that a flower does not exist independently but is the result of various conditions such as sunlight, soil, and water. Recognizing this interconnectedness reveals the true nature of the flower as empty of a separate, permanent essence. This understanding helps individuals see beyond the illusions of separateness and permanence.

Nishitani's focus on emptiness offers valuable insights for both philosophical and spiritual exploration. His teachings encourage a deeper awareness of the interconnectedness of all things and the impermanent nature of existence, fostering a more mindful and liberated way of living.

SEPTEMBER 23: NISHITANI KEIJI - EXISTENTIAL PHILOSOPHY: ADDRESSING LIFE'S FUNDAMENTAL QUESTIONS

NISHITANI KEIJI'S EXISTENTIAL PHILOSOPHY addresses life's fundamental questions about meaning, purpose, and the nature of existence. He combined existentialist themes with Zen insights to explore how individuals can find meaning in a seemingly indifferent or absurd universe. Nishitani believed that confronting and embracing the void leads to genuine self-discovery and spiritual fulfillment.

Nishitani used the example of personal crisis to illustrate his approach. He argued that crises, such as loss or existential doubt, force individuals to confront the emptiness at the core of their existence. By embracing this emptiness rather than fleeing from it, individuals can transform their understanding of themselves and the world, leading to a deeper and more authentic existence.

Nishitani's existential philosophy offers a unique perspective on the human condition, bridging Eastern and Western traditions. His ideas provide practical and profound guidance for those seeking to navigate the complexities of life and to find deeper meaning and purpose.

September 24: Erich Fromm - Escape from Freedom: Analysis of Modern Society

E RICH FROMM, A GERMAN social psychologist and philosopher, explored the dynamics of freedom and authority in his work "Escape from Freedom." Fromm analyzed how modern society, while offering more individual freedom, also creates conditions that lead to feelings of isolation and powerlessness. He argued that many people escape from the burden of freedom by conforming to authoritarian structures or losing themselves in consumerism.

Fromm used the example of fascism to illustrate his theory. He argued that the rise of fascism in the 20th century was partly due to individuals' desire to escape the uncertainties and responsibilities of freedom by submitting to authoritarian leaders who promised security and identity. This dynamic reveals the psychological challenges associated with modern freedom.

Fromm's analysis of freedom has influenced social and political thought, highlighting the psychological aspects of authority and conformity. His ideas encourage a deeper understanding of the balance between individual freedom and societal pressures.

SEPTEMBER 25: ERICH FROMM - THE ART OF LOVING: IMPORTANCE OF LOVE IN HUMAN LIFE

I N "THE ART OF Loving," Erich Fromm emphasized the importance of love as a fundamental human need and a key to achieving personal fulfillment and social harmony. Fromm argued that love is an art that requires knowledge, effort, and practice, rather than just an emotional state. He identified different forms of love, including romantic love, brotherly love, and self-love, each contributing to a person's overall well-being.

Fromm used the example of self-love to illustrate his point. He argued that genuine self-love is not selfishness but a healthy respect and care for oneself, which enables one to love others more fully. This balance between self-love and love for others is essential for healthy relationships and personal growth.

Fromm's insights on love have had a lasting impact on psychology and social theory, emphasizing the transformative power of love in human life. His ideas continue to inspire efforts to cultivate more loving and compassionate relationships and societies.

SEPTEMBER 26: ERICH FROMM - SOCIAL PSYCHOLOGY: INFLUENCE OF SOCIETY ON INDIVIDUAL

FROMM'S WORK IN SOCIAL psychology explores how societal structures and cultural norms shape individual behavior, thoughts, and feelings. He believed that understanding these influences is crucial for addressing psychological and social issues. Fromm argued that modern capitalist society, with its emphasis on material success and competition, often leads to alienation and dehumanization.

Fromm used the example of consumer culture to illustrate the influence of society on the individual. He argued that the constant pursuit of material goods and status, driven by societal pressures, often leads to a sense of emptiness and dissatisfaction. This focus on external validation undermines genuine self-worth and personal fulfillment.

Fromm's contributions to social psychology have provided valuable insights into the interplay between individual psychology and social structures. His ideas encourage a critical examination of societal norms and their impact on personal and collective well-being.

September 27: Theodor W. Adorno - Critical Theory

T HEODOR W. ADORNO, A German philosopher and sociologist, was a leading figure in the Frankfurt School
of Critical Theory. Critical Theory seeks to understand and
critique society by uncovering the power dynamics and ideologies that shape it. Adorno believed that critical thought
is essential for challenging oppressive structures and promoting human emancipation.

Adorno used the example of mass culture to illustrate Critical Theory. He argued that mass-produced culture, such as
popular music and movies, reinforces capitalist ideologies
and suppresses critical thinking. By providing standardized entertainment, mass culture distracts people from the
realities of their exploitation and limits their capacity for
resistance.

Adorno's work in Critical Theory has influenced a wide
range of fields, including sociology, cultural studies, and political science. His ideas encourage a deeper analysis of the
cultural and ideological forces that shape society, promoting
a more critical and emancipatory approach to understanding the world.

SEPTEMBER 28: THEODOR W. ADORNO - CULTURE INDUSTRY

A DORNO, ALONG WITH MAX Horkheimer, introduced the concept of the culture industry in their work "Dialectic of Enlightenment." The culture industry refers to the mass production of cultural goods, such as films, music, and television, which Adorno argued serve to manipulate and pacify the public. This industrialization of culture standardizes and commodifies artistic expression, reducing its potential for critical reflection and resistance.

Adorno used the example of popular music to illustrate the culture industry. He argued that the repetitive and formulaic nature of popular music promotes passive consumption rather than active engagement. This standardization of culture creates a homogeneous and compliant audience, undermining the potential for genuine creativity and critical thought.

Adorno's concept of the culture industry has had a profound impact on media studies and cultural criticism, highlighting the ways in which mass media can shape and control public consciousness. His ideas encourage a more critical and reflective engagement with cultural products.

September 29: Theodor W. Adorno - Negative Dialectics

A DORNO'S "NEGATIVE DIALECTICS" REPRESENTS a critical approach to traditional dialectical thinking, particularly Hegelian dialectics. While Hegel's dialectics aimed at synthesizing contradictions into a unified whole, Adorno's negative dialectics emphasizes the persistence of contradictions and the impossibility of achieving total reconciliation. Adorno believed that acknowledging and engaging with these contradictions is essential for genuine critical thought.

Adorno used the example of social inequalities to illustrate negative dialectics. He argued that instead of attempting to reconcile or justify social inequalities through abstract theories, critical thought should expose and confront these contradictions, highlighting the ways in which they reflect deeper structural issues in society.

Adorno's negative dialectics has influenced contemporary philosophy and critical theory, promoting a more nuanced and critical approach to understanding social and philosophical issues. His ideas challenge the pursuit of simplistic resolutions, encouraging a deeper engagement with the complexities and contradictions of reality.

September 30: Jean-Paul Sartre - Existentialism: Existence Precedes Essence

JEAN-PAUL SARTRE, A FRENCH existentialist philosopher, is best known for his assertion that "existence precedes essence." Sartre argued that individuals are not born with a predetermined nature or purpose; instead, they must create their own essence through their actions and choices. This emphasis on radical freedom and self-determination is central to existentialist thought.

Sartre used the example of a paper cutter to illustrate his philosophy. Unlike a paper cutter, which is designed for a specific purpose, human beings are not created with an inherent purpose. Instead, individuals must define their own purpose through their actions and decisions. This freedom to create oneself is both empowering and burdensome, as it entails full responsibility for one's existence.

Sartre's existentialism has profoundly influenced philosophy, literature, and psychology, emphasizing the importance of individual freedom and the responsibility that comes with it. His ideas challenge traditional notions of human nature and purpose, promoting a more dynamic and self-determined approach to life.

October 1: Jean-Paul Sartre - Bad Faith: Denial of One's Freedom

S ARTRE ALSO INTRODUCED THE concept of "bad faith," which refers to the denial or avoidance of one's inherent freedom and responsibility. Bad faith occurs when individuals deceive themselves into believing that they are not free to make choices, often by conforming to societal roles or expectations. This self-deception undermines authentic existence and personal growth.

Sartre used the example of a waiter to illustrate bad faith. A waiter who overly identifies with his role, acting as if his existence is entirely defined by his job, is in bad faith. By denying his freedom to choose other possibilities, he limits his potential and authenticity. This behavior reflects a refusal to confront the anxiety and responsibility of freedom.

Sartre's concept of bad faith has influenced existential psychology and ethics, highlighting the importance of embracing one's freedom and responsibility. His ideas encourage individuals to live more authentically, acknowledging and exercising their capacity for choice.

October 2: Jean-Paul Sartre - Radical Freedom and Responsibility

C ENTRAL TO SARTRE'S PHILOSOPHY is the idea of radical freedom, which posits that individuals are entirely free to make their own choices and create their own values. With this freedom comes profound responsibility, as individuals must bear the consequences of their actions and the burden of shaping their own existence.

Sartre used the example of moral decision-making to illustrate radical freedom. He argued that in making moral choices, individuals cannot rely on external authorities or predefined values; they must create their own ethical frameworks and take full responsibility for their decisions. This process requires courage and a willingness to confront the uncertainties of life.

Sartre's emphasis on radical freedom and responsibility has influenced existentialist ethics and political thought, promoting a vision of human beings as autonomous and self-determining agents. His ideas challenge individuals to embrace their freedom and to live with integrity and purpose.

OCTOBER 3: HANNAH ARENDT - THE HUMAN CONDITION: VITA ACTIVA AND VITA CONTEMPLATIVA

H ANNAH ARENDT, A GERMAN-AMERICAN philosopher and political theorist, explored the nature of human activities in her seminal work "The Human Condition."
She distinguished between vita activa (active life) and vita
contemplativa (contemplative life), arguing that both are essential to human existence. Vita activa includes labor, work,
and action, while vita contemplativa involves thinking, reflecting, and seeking understanding.

Arendt used the example of political action to illustrate vita
activa. She argued that participating in public affairs and
engaging in political discourse are fundamental aspects of
the active life, contributing to the shared world and collective human experience. This engagement contrasts with the
more solitary and introspective nature of the contemplative
life.

Arendt's analysis of the human condition has influenced political theory and philosophy, highlighting the importance
of balancing action and contemplation. Her ideas encourage
a more holistic understanding of human life, recognizing
the value of both public engagement and private reflection.

October 4: Hannah Arendt - Totalitarianism: Analysis of Authoritarian Regimes

I N HER INFLUENTIAL WORK "The Origins of Totalitarianism," Arendt examined the nature and origins of totalitarian regimes, focusing on Nazi Germany and Stalinist Russia. She identified key characteristics of totalitarianism, such as the use of terror, propaganda, and ideology to control and manipulate populations. Arendt argued that totalitarianism seeks to dominate every aspect of life, erasing individuality and freedom.

Arendt used the example of propaganda to illustrate the mechanisms of totalitarian control. She argued that totalitarian regimes employ propaganda to create a distorted reality, shaping public perception and eliminating dissent. This manipulation undermines truth and fosters an environment of fear and conformity.

Arendt's analysis of totalitarianism has had a profound impact on political science and history, providing valuable insights into the dynamics of authoritarian regimes. Her ideas continue to inform discussions on the threats to democracy and the importance of protecting individual rights and freedoms.

OCTOBER 5: HANNAH ARENDT - THE BANALITY OF EVIL: ORDINARY PEOPLE AND ATROCITIES

A RENDT INTRODUCED THE CONCEPT of the "banality of evil" in her report on the trial of Adolf Eichmann, a Nazi official responsible for organizing the Holocaust. Arendt argued that Eichmann was not a monstrous, fanatical figure but an ordinary, bureaucratic individual who simply followed orders without critical reflection. This idea challenges conventional views of evil as the domain of inherently malevolent individuals.

Arendt used the example of Eichmann's defense to illustrate the banality of evil. Eichmann claimed he was merely following orders and doing his duty, without considering the moral implications of his actions. This lack of critical thinking and moral responsibility, Arendt argued, is what enables ordinary people to commit horrific atrocities.

Arendt's concept of the banality of evil has influenced moral and political philosophy, prompting a reevaluation of how we understand and judge acts of evil. Her ideas highlight the importance of individual responsibility and the dangers of unreflective conformity.

OCTOBER 6: IMMANUEL LEVINAS - ETHICS AS FIRST PHILOSOPHY

I MMANUEL LEVINAS, A FRENCH philosopher of Lithuanian-Jewish descent, argued that ethics should be the primary focus of philosophy. He believed that the fundamental philosophical question is not about being or knowledge, but about our responsibility to the Other. Levinas emphasized the ethical encounter with the Other as the foundation of all human relationships and philosophical inquiry.

Levinas used the example of a face-to-face encounter to illustrate his ethical philosophy. He argued that when we encounter another person, their face reveals their vulnerability and demands an ethical response. This encounter challenges us to recognize and respect the humanity of the Other, placing ethical responsibility at the center of our existence.

Levinas's emphasis on ethics as first philosophy has influenced contemporary ethical theory and existentialism, highlighting the primacy of human relationships and moral responsibility. His ideas challenge us to prioritize ethical considerations in our interactions and philosophical explorations.

October 7: Immanuel Levinas - Face-to-Face Encounter

L EVINAS'S CONCEPT OF THE face-to-face encounter is central to his ethical philosophy. He argued that the face of the Other calls us to ethical responsibility, revealing their vulnerability and humanity. This encounter transcends cognitive understanding and invokes a direct, ethical relationship that requires us to respond with compassion and respect.

Levinas used the example of helping a stranger to illustrate the face-to-face encounter. When we see someone in need, their face calls upon us to act ethically, not out of obligation or calculation, but from a direct recognition of their humanity. This immediate ethical response forms the basis of genuine moral action.

Levinas's focus on the face-to-face encounter has had a significant impact on ethical and existential philosophy, emphasizing the importance of personal relationships and ethical responsibility. His ideas encourage a deeper engagement with the ethical dimensions of our interactions with others.

October 8: Immanuel Levinas - The Other and Infinite Responsibility

L EVINAS ARGUED THAT OUR ethical responsibility to the Other is infinite and unending. This responsibility is not based on mutual agreement or reciprocity but is an unconditional and limitless obligation that arises from the encounter with the Other. Levinas believed that this infinite responsibility defines our humanity and guides our ethical actions.

Levinas used the example of hospitality to illustrate infinite responsibility. He argued that welcoming and caring for strangers without expecting anything in return reflects the infinite nature of ethical responsibility. This hospitality extends beyond mere duty, embodying a profound respect for the Other's dignity and humanity.

Levinas's concept of infinite responsibility has influenced contemporary ethical thought, challenging us to reconsider the nature and scope of our moral obligations. His ideas promote a more compassionate and selfless approach to ethics, recognizing the endless demands of our responsibility to others.

October 9: H.L.A. Hart - Legal Positivism: Separation of Law and Morality

H .L.A. HART, A BRITISH legal philosopher, is best known for his contributions to legal positivism, a theory that emphasizes the separation of law and morality. Hart argued that legal systems are based on social rules and conventions, not on moral principles. According to Hart, laws are valid if they are enacted according to the rules and procedures of a legal system, regardless of their moral content.

Hart used the example of a traffic law to illustrate legal positivism. He argued that a law requiring drivers to stop at red lights is valid because it follows the legal procedures, not because it is morally right. This separation allows for a clear distinction between what the law is and what it ought to be, enabling a more objective analysis of legal systems.

Hart's legal positivism has significantly influenced legal theory, promoting a more analytical and descriptive approach to understanding law. His ideas challenge the notion that law must inherently be tied to morality, emphasizing the importance of legal structures and procedures.

October 10: H.L.A. Hart - The Concept of Law: Analysis of Legal Systems

I N HIS SEMINAL WORK "The Concept of Law," H.L.A. Hart provided a detailed analysis of legal systems, focusing on the nature and function of law. Hart introduced the idea of law as a system of rules, distinguishing between primary rules, which govern behavior, and secondary rules, which provide the methods for creating, changing, and interpreting primary rules.

Hart used the example of a constitution to illustrate his analysis. He argued that a constitution serves as a secondary rule that outlines the procedures for enacting and amending laws. This framework allows for a stable and adaptable legal system, capable of responding to changing social needs and circumstances.

Hart's analysis of legal systems has had a profound impact on jurisprudence, offering a comprehensive and systematic approach to understanding the structure and function of law. His ideas continue to influence contemporary legal scholarship and practice.

October 11: H.L.A. Hart - Rules: Primary and Secondary

H ART'S DISTINCTION BETWEEN PRIMARY and secondary rules is a cornerstone of his legal theory. Primary rules are the basic rules that govern behavior, while secondary rules are the rules about the rules, providing the mechanisms for creating, modifying, and adjudicating primary rules. This distinction allows for a more nuanced understanding of legal systems and their operation.

Hart used the example of contract law to illustrate primary and secondary rules. Primary rules would be the specific laws governing contracts, such as requirements for a valid contract. Secondary rules would include the procedures for resolving contract disputes and the methods for changing contract law.

Hart's distinction between primary and secondary rules has influenced legal theory by highlighting the complexity and multi-layered nature of legal systems. His ideas encourage a more detailed and structured analysis of how laws are created, implemented, and enforced.

OCTOBER 12: SIMONE DE BEAUVOIR - FEMINISM: GENDER AS A SOCIAL CONSTRUCT

S IMONE DE BEAUVOIR, A French existentialist philosopher and feminist, argued that gender is a social construct rather than a biological given. In her groundbreaking
work "The Second Sex," de Beauvoir examined how society
constructs and perpetuates gender roles, limiting women's
freedom and opportunities. She famously declared, "One is
not born, but rather becomes, a woman," emphasizing the
role of socialization in shaping gender identity.

De Beauvoir used the example of childhood socialization to
illustrate her point. She argued that from a young age, girls
are taught to conform to feminine ideals, such as passivity
and nurturing, while boys are encouraged to be assertive
and independent. This social conditioning reinforces gender stereotypes and restricts individual potential.

De Beauvoir's insights on gender as a social construct have
had a profound impact on feminist theory and gender studies. Her ideas challenge traditional notions of gender, advocating for greater equality and freedom for all individuals,
regardless of their gender.

October 13: Simone de Beauvoir - The Second Sex: Women's Oppression

I N "THE SECOND SEX," Simone de Beauvoir explored the historical and social factors that contribute to women's oppression. She examined how women have been marginalized and objectified throughout history, treated as the "other" in a male-dominated society. De Beauvoir argued that women's liberation requires a radical restructuring of social, economic, and cultural institutions.

De Beauvoir used the example of women's economic dependence on men to illustrate their oppression. She argued that women's lack of access to education and employment opportunities forces them to rely on men for financial support, perpetuating their subordination. Achieving economic independence is crucial for women's emancipation.

De Beauvoir's analysis of women's oppression has had a lasting impact on feminist movements worldwide, inspiring efforts to address gender inequality and promote women's rights. Her work continues to be a foundational text in feminist philosophy and social theory.

OCTOBER 14: SIMONE DE BEAUVOIR - EXISTENTIAL ETHICS: FREEDOM AND RESPONSIBILITY

S IMONE DE BEAUVOIR'S EXISTENTIAL ethics emphasize the importance of freedom and responsibility in
human life. She argued that individuals must create their
own values and meanings through their choices and actions,
embracing their freedom and taking responsibility for their
impact on others. This ethical framework is closely tied to
her existentialist philosophy, which posits that existence
precedes essence.

De Beauvoir used the example of personal relationships to
illustrate existential ethics. She argued that in genuine relationships, individuals must recognize and respect each other's freedom, avoiding manipulation and domination. This
mutual respect fosters authentic connections and ethical
interactions.

De Beauvoir's existential ethics have influenced contemporary moral philosophy, highlighting the interplay between freedom, responsibility, and interpersonal relationships. Her ideas encourage individuals to live authentically
and ethically, embracing their freedom and the responsibilities that come with it.

October 15: W.V.O. Quine - Ontological Relativity: Context-Dependent Meaning

W.V.O. QUINE, AN AMERICAN philosopher and logician, introduced the concept of ontological relativity, arguing that the meaning of terms and the existence of entities are dependent on the conceptual schemes we use. Quine believed that our understanding of the world is shaped by the linguistic and theoretical frameworks we adopt, making meaning and existence context-dependent.

Quine used the example of scientific theories to illustrate ontological relativity. He argued that the entities posited by different scientific theories, such as electrons in physics or genes in biology, are meaningful only within the context of those theories. This perspective challenges the notion of an objective reality independent of our conceptual schemes.

Quine's concept of ontological relativity has influenced philosophy of language and metaphysics, emphasizing the interplay between language, theory, and reality. His ideas encourage a more flexible and context-sensitive approach to understanding meaning and existence.

October 16: W.V.O. Quine - The Indeterminacy of Translation: Incompatible Meanings

Q UINE ALSO EXPLORED THE indeterminacy of translation, the idea that there are no unique, correct translations between different languages because of inherent ambiguities and differences in conceptual schemes. He argued that meaning is not fixed but varies depending on the linguistic and cultural context, making exact translation impossible.

Quine used the example of translating the word "gavagai" from a hypothetical language to illustrate the indeterminacy of translation. He argued that without knowing the underlying conceptual scheme, "gavagai" could be translated as "rabbit," "undetached rabbit parts," or "rabbit stage." This ambiguity highlights the challenges of achieving precise translation and understanding.

Quine's exploration of the indeterminacy of translation has had a significant impact on philosophy of language and linguistic theory, emphasizing the complexities of meaning and communication across different languages and cultures. His ideas challenge assumptions about the universality of meaning and encourage a more nuanced understanding of linguistic diversity.

October 17: W.V.O. Quine - Naturalized Epistemology: Knowledge through Empirical Science

QUINE ADVOCATED FOR NATURALIZED epistemology, the view that epistemological questions about knowledge and justification should be addressed using empirical methods from the natural sciences. He believed that traditional philosophical approaches to epistemology, which relied on abstract analysis and intuition, were inadequate and should be replaced by a more scientific approach.

Quine used the example of sensory perception to illustrate naturalized epistemology. He argued that understanding how we acquire knowledge should involve studying the biological and psychological processes underlying perception and cognition. This empirical investigation provides a more reliable foundation for epistemology than speculative philosophical theories.

Quine's naturalized epistemology has influenced contemporary epistemology and philosophy of science, promoting a more interdisciplinary and empirical approach to understanding knowledge. His ideas encourage collaboration between philosophy and the natural sciences to address fundamental questions about human cognition and understanding.

OCTOBER 18: MAURICE MERLEAU-PONTY - PHENOMENOLOGY OF PERCEPTION: EMBODIED EXPERIENCE

MAURICE MERLEAU-PONTY, A FRENCH phenome-nologist, emphasized the importance of embodied experience in understanding human perception and consciousness. In his work "Phenomenology of Perception," Merleau-Ponty argued that our bodily experience is fundamental to how we perceive and interact with the world, challenging the Cartesian dualism of mind and body.

Merleau-Ponty used the example of spatial awareness to illustrate embodied perception. He argued that our understanding of space is rooted in our bodily movements and sensations, such as reaching for objects or navigating our environment. This embodied perspective contrasts with the abstract, disembodied view of perception that focuses solely on mental representations.

Merleau-Ponty's emphasis on embodied experience has influenced phenomenology, cognitive science, and philosophy of mind, highlighting the interdependence of body and mind in shaping human experience. His ideas encourage a more integrated and holistic approach to understanding perception and consciousness.

October 19: Maurice Merleau-Ponty - The Primacy of Perception: Foundation of Knowledge

MERLEAU-PONTY ARGUED FOR THE primacy of perception, asserting that perception is the foundational basis of all knowledge. He believed that our direct, pre-reflective experience of the world precedes and grounds all cognitive and conceptual knowledge. This perspective challenges the traditional view that knowledge is primarily derived from abstract reasoning and analysis.

Merleau-Ponty used the example of a child learning to walk to illustrate the primacy of perception. He argued that the child's understanding of balance and movement is rooted in their direct bodily experience, not in conscious deliberation or abstract concepts. This primary experience forms the basis for further cognitive development and understanding.

Merleau-Ponty's emphasis on the primacy of perception has influenced phenomenology and epistemology, promoting a more experiential and embodied approach to knowledge. His ideas highlight the importance of direct experience in shaping our understanding of the world.

October 20: Maurice Merleau-Ponty - Intertwining of Subject and Object

MERLEAU-PONTY INTRODUCED THE CONCEPT of the intertwining of subject and object, arguing that the distinction between the perceiving subject and the perceived object is not absolute but interrelated. He believed that our perception of the world involves a dynamic interaction between our embodied selves and our environment, challenging the traditional separation of subject and object.

Merleau-Ponty used the example of holding an object to illustrate this concept. He argued that when we hold an object, such as a tool, it becomes an extension of our body, blurring the line between subject and object. This interaction reflects the inseparability of our perception and the world we perceive.

Merleau-Ponty's concept of the intertwining of subject and object has influenced existentialism, phenomenology, and cognitive science, encouraging a more integrated understanding of human perception and experience. His ideas challenge the rigid distinctions between self and world, promoting a more holistic view of our interaction with reality.

OCTOBER 21: SIMONE WEIL - ATTENTION: FOCUSED ATTENTION AS A MORAL ACT

S IMONE WEIL, A FRENCH philosopher and mystic, emphasized the moral and spiritual significance of attention. She argued that focused attention is not only a cognitive process but also an ethical act that involves fully acknowledging and responding to the reality of others. Weil believed that true attention requires a suspension of the self and a deep receptivity to the needs and experiences of others.

Weil used the example of listening to someone in distress to illustrate the moral act of attention. She argued that by giving our undivided attention to another person's suffering, we recognize their humanity and offer genuine compassion. This attentive presence fosters a deeper connection and understanding, reflecting an ethical commitment to others.

Weil's emphasis on attention has influenced ethical philosophy and spiritual practice, highlighting the transformative power of focused, compassionate awareness. Her ideas encourage a more mindful and ethically engaged approach to our interactions with others.

October 22: Simone Weil - Affliction: Understanding Suffering and its Spiritual Significance

W EIL ALSO EXPLORED THE concept of affliction, viewing it as a profound form of suffering that affects the body, mind, and soul. She believed that understanding and embracing affliction can lead to spiritual growth and transformation. Weil saw affliction as an opportunity to confront the deeper aspects of human existence and to cultivate empathy and compassion for others.

Weil used the example of physical illness to illustrate affliction. She argued that illness forces individuals to confront their vulnerability and limitations, stripping away illusions of control and self-sufficiency. This experience can lead to a deeper understanding of suffering and a greater capacity for empathy and solidarity with others who suffer.

Weil's insights into affliction have influenced existential and spiritual philosophy, offering a profound perspective on the role of suffering in human life. Her ideas encourage a more compassionate and spiritually aware approach to understanding and addressing suffering.

October 23: Simone Weil - Labor: Spiritual Value in Work and Toil

S IMONE WEIL PLACED A significant emphasis on the spiritual value of labor and toil. She believed that work, when approached with the right mindset, can be a path to spiritual growth and self-transcendence. Weil argued that by engaging fully and mindfully in our work, we can cultivate virtues such as patience, humility, and dedication.

Weil used the example of manual labor to illustrate the spiritual value of work. She argued that tasks such as farming or factory work, often seen as menial, can become acts of devotion and discipline when performed with care and attention. This perspective transforms work into a meaningful and spiritually enriching activity.

Weil's views on labor have influenced discussions on the ethics of work and the spiritual dimensions of everyday activities. Her ideas encourage a more mindful and appreciative approach to our daily tasks, recognizing the potential for spiritual growth in even the most mundane activities.

October 24: A.J. Ayer - Logical Positivism: Verification Principle

A .J. AYER, A BRITISH philosopher, was a leading proponent of logical positivism, a philosophical movement that emphasized the verification principle. According to this principle, a statement is meaningful only if it can be empirically verified or is analytically true. Ayer argued that many traditional philosophical questions, particularly those related to metaphysics and theology, are meaningless because they cannot be empirically verified.

Ayer used the example of a scientific hypothesis to illustrate the verification principle. He argued that a hypothesis is meaningful because it can be tested and confirmed or refuted through empirical observation. In contrast, statements about the existence of God or the nature of the soul are not empirically verifiable and therefore lack cognitive meaning.

Ayer's logical positivism has influenced contemporary philosophy, particularly in the philosophy of language and the philosophy of science. His ideas challenge traditional metaphysical and theological claims, promoting a more empirical and scientific approach to philosophical inquiry.

October 25: A.J. Ayer - Language, Truth, and Logic: Analysis of Language

I N HIS SEMINAL WORK "Language, Truth, and Logic," A.J. Ayer analyzed the nature of language and its relation to truth and logic. Ayer argued that philosophical problems often arise from misunderstandings and misuses of language. He believed that by clarifying the logical structure of language, many philosophical issues could be resolved or dissolved.

Ayer used the example of ethical statements to illustrate his analysis. He argued that statements such as "Murder is wrong" are not factual claims but expressions of emotion and attitude. This view, known as emotivism, suggests that ethical statements cannot be true or false in the same way that factual statements can.

Ayer's analysis of language has had a significant impact on analytic philosophy, promoting a more rigorous and logical approach to understanding language and meaning. His ideas encourage a critical examination of how language shapes our philosophical concepts and discussions.

October 26: A.J. Ayer - Emotivism: Moral Statements as Expressions of Emotion

AYER'S EMOTIVISM IS A key component of his ethical philosophy, asserting that moral statements do not describe facts but express the speaker's emotions and attitudes. According to emotivism, saying "Stealing is wrong" is equivalent to expressing disapproval of stealing, rather than stating an objective fact about stealing.

Ayer used the example of a debate on morality to illustrate emotivism. He argued that when people argue about moral issues, they are not debating factual matters but expressing their feelings and attempting to influence others' attitudes. This perspective challenges the idea that moral statements can be true or false in the same way as factual statements.

Ayer's emotivism has influenced meta-ethics and the philosophy of language, offering a distinctive view on the nature of moral discourse. His ideas encourage a reexamination of how we understand and discuss ethical issues, focusing on the expressive and persuasive aspects of moral language.

October 27: J.L. Austin - Speech Act Theory: How Words Do Things

J.L. Austin, a British philosopher, developed Speech Act Theory, which examines how language is used to perform actions rather than merely to convey information. Austin argued that many utterances are not simply statements but performative acts that accomplish something in the world, such as promising, ordering, or apologizing.

Austin used the example of a wedding ceremony to illustrate speech acts. When someone says "I do" during a wedding, they are not merely stating a fact but performing the act of marrying. This utterance creates a new social reality, demonstrating how language can be used to enact change.

Austin's Speech Act Theory has had a significant impact on the philosophy of language and linguistics, highlighting the performative aspects of language. His ideas encourage a more dynamic and practical understanding of how language functions in everyday life.

October 28: J.L. Austin - Performative Utterances: Language as Action

A USTIN INTRODUCED THE CONCEPT of performative utterances, which are statements that do not merely describe a situation but perform a specific action. Performative utterances, such as promises, apologies, and commands, are effective because they fulfill the action they describe at the moment of utterance.

Austin used the example of making a promise to illustrate performative utterances. When someone says "I promise to meet you tomorrow," they are not just reporting an intention but actively committing to a future action. The utterance itself creates the obligation, demonstrating how language can shape social interactions.

Austin's focus on performative utterances has influenced various fields, including linguistics, communication studies, and philosophy of language. His ideas emphasize the active and social dimensions of language, showing how speech can be a form of action that impacts the world.

OCTOBER 29: J.L. AUSTIN - ORDINARY LANGUAGE PHILOSOPHY: ANALYZING EVERYDAY LANGUAGE

A USTIN WAS A LEADING figure in Ordinary Language Philosophy, which advocates for analyzing everyday language to understand philosophical problems. He believed that many philosophical confusions arise from misunderstandings of ordinary language and that by examining how words are used in everyday contexts, we can clarify and resolve these issues.

Austin used the example of the word "know" to illustrate Ordinary Language Philosophy. He argued that philosophical debates about knowledge often overlook the various ways people use "know" in daily conversation. By examining these everyday uses, we can gain a clearer understanding of what it means to "know" something and avoid abstract, misleading definitions.

Austin's Ordinary Language Philosophy has influenced contemporary analytic philosophy, promoting a more grounded and practical approach to philosophical analysis. His ideas encourage philosophers to pay closer attention to the nuances of everyday language, fostering a more precise and context-sensitive understanding of philosophical concepts.

October 30: Leopoldo Zea - Philosophy of Liberation: Emancipation of Latin America from Colonial Thought

L EOPOLDO ZEA, A MEXICAN philosopher, focused on the philosophy of liberation, aiming to emancipate Latin American thought from the legacy of colonialism. Zea argued that Latin America needed to develop its own philosophical identity, free from the intellectual dominance of European colonial powers. He believed that this process involved critically examining and rejecting colonial ideologies that had shaped Latin American societies.

Zea used the example of cultural syncretism in Latin America to illustrate his philosophy. He argued that Latin American cultures are a blend of indigenous, African, and European influences. By embracing this unique cultural identity, Latin Americans could resist colonial ideologies and create a new, independent philosophical perspective.

Zea's philosophy of liberation has influenced Latin American thought, promoting intellectual and cultural independence. His ideas encourage a critical examination of colonial legacies and the development of a distinct Latin American philosophical identity.

October 31: Leopoldo Zea - Cultural Identity: Latin American Identity and its Philosophical Implications

Z EA EMPHASIZED THE IMPORTANCE of cultural identity in shaping Latin American philosophy. He believed that understanding and embracing Latin American cultural identity was crucial for developing a philosophical framework that reflected the region's unique historical and social experiences. Zea argued that this cultural identity should be celebrated and explored in philosophical discourse.

Zea used the example of Latin American literature to illustrate the role of cultural identity. He pointed out that works by authors like Gabriel García Márquez and Octavio Paz capture the essence of Latin American life, blending magical realism with social and political commentary. This literature reflects a distinct cultural perspective that can inform and enrich philosophical thought.

Zea's focus on cultural identity has influenced contemporary Latin American philosophy, encouraging a deeper exploration of the region's cultural and intellectual heritage. His ideas highlight the importance of integrating cultural identity into philosophical inquiry.

November 1: Leopoldo Zea - Critique of Eurocentrism: Challenge to European Dominance in Philosophy

Z EA'S CRITIQUE OF EUROCENTRISM was central to his philosophical project. He argued that European philosophy had dominated intellectual discourse for too long, marginalizing other perspectives, particularly those from Latin America. Zea called for a rejection of Eurocentrism and the recognition of diverse philosophical traditions.

Zea used the example of indigenous knowledge systems to illustrate his critique. He argued that indigenous philosophies, with their deep understanding of nature and community, offer valuable insights that are often overlooked by Eurocentric frameworks. By incorporating these perspectives, philosophy can become more inclusive and comprehensive.

Zea's critique of Eurocentrism has contributed to the decolonization of philosophy, promoting a more pluralistic and inclusive approach. His ideas encourage the recognition and integration of diverse philosophical traditions from around the world.

NOVEMBER 2: WILFRID SELLARS - SCIENTIFIC IMAGE VS. MANIFEST IMAGE: DIFFERENT WAYS OF VIEWING THE WORLD

W ILFRID SELLARS, AN AMERICAN philosopher, distinguished between the "scientific image" and the "manifest image" of the world. The scientific image refers to the world as described by science, with its emphasis on objective, empirical knowledge. The manifest image, on the other hand, encompasses the world as experienced by humans, including everyday perceptions and interactions.

Sellars used the example of perception to illustrate this distinction. Scientifically, perception involves the processing of sensory data by the brain. However, in the manifest image, perception is experienced as seeing objects in the world. Sellars argued that both images are essential for a complete understanding of human experience, as they represent different aspects of reality.

Sellars' distinction between the scientific and manifest images has influenced philosophy of mind and epistemology, encouraging a more integrated approach to understanding reality. His ideas highlight the importance of considering both scientific and experiential perspectives.

NOVEMBER 3: WILFRID SELLARS - MYTH OF THE GIVEN: CRITIQUE OF FOUNDATIONALISM

S ELLARS' CRITIQUE OF THE "Myth of the Given" is a central aspect of his philosophy. He argued against the idea that knowledge can be based on a foundation of indubitable, pre-conceptual experiences or "givens." Sellars believed that all knowledge is theory-laden, shaped by conceptual frameworks and inferential processes.

Sellars used the example of sense-data theories to illustrate his critique. He argued that the idea of raw, uninterpreted sense-data as a basis for knowledge is flawed because our perceptions are always influenced by prior knowledge and conceptual understanding. This challenges the notion that there are pure, foundational experiences from which knowledge can be built.

Sellars' critique of the Myth of the Given has influenced contemporary epistemology, promoting a more holistic and coherentist approach to knowledge. His ideas encourage a reevaluation of how we understand and justify our beliefs.

November 4: Wilfrid Sellars - Functional Role: Understanding Mental States

S ELLARS INTRODUCED THE IDEA of understanding mental states through their functional roles within a network of relations. He argued that mental states should not be viewed as isolated, inner experiences but as parts of a system of interactions that include behavior, environmental stimuli, and other mental states.

Sellars used the example of belief to illustrate the functional role approach. He argued that a belief is defined by its role in influencing behavior and other mental states, such as desires and intentions. This functional understanding emphasizes the relational and dynamic nature of mental states.

Sellars' functional role approach has influenced the philosophy of mind and cognitive science, promoting a more systematic and interactional understanding of mental processes. His ideas challenge traditional views of mental states as private, introspective entities, encouraging a broader perspective on cognition and behavior.

November 5: Albert Camus - Absurdism: Life's Inherent Meaninglessness

A LBERT CAMUS, A FRENCH-ALGERIAN philosopher and writer, is known for his philosophy of absurdism, which confronts the inherent meaninglessness of life. Camus argued that the human search for meaning in an indifferent universe leads to a fundamental conflict, or "the absurd." This conflict arises from the juxtaposition of humans' desire for significance and the universe's indifference.

Camus used the example of the myth of Sisyphus to illustrate absurdism. Sisyphus, condemned to eternally roll a boulder up a hill only for it to roll back down, symbolizes the human condition. Despite the futility of his task, Sisyphus continues to push the boulder, representing the persistence of human effort in the face of meaninglessness.

Camus' absurdism has influenced existential philosophy and literature, encouraging individuals to confront and embrace the absurd. His ideas challenge us to find meaning and joy in life despite its inherent lack of purpose.

November 6: Albert Camus - The Myth of Sisyphus: Embrace the Absurd

IN "THE MYTH OF Sisyphus," Camus elaborates on his philosophy of absurdism, suggesting that we must embrace the absurd and find meaning within it. He argued that recognizing the absurdity of life does not lead to despair but rather to a form of liberation. By accepting the absurd, we can live more fully and authentically.

Camus used the story of Sisyphus to illustrate this embrace. He argued that Sisyphus' awareness of his futile task and his continued effort embody the human spirit's resilience. Sisyphus' defiance in the face of absurdity becomes a source of meaning and strength, transforming his punishment into a triumph of human will.

Camus' message of embracing the absurd has inspired existentialist thought and literature, encouraging a courageous and defiant approach to life's challenges. His ideas promote a philosophy of action and engagement, even in the face of life's inherent meaninglessness.

NOVEMBER 7: ALBERT CAMUS - REVOLT: FINDING MEANING DESPITE THE ABSURD

C AMUS ADVOCATED FOR REVOLT as a way to find meaning and purpose in an absurd world. Revolt involves a conscious rejection of despair and a commitment to live authentically and passionately. For Camus, this revolt is not a call to violence but a personal stance of defiance against the absurd.

Camus used the example of his own life to illustrate the concept of revolt. Despite facing the absurdity of existence, he chose to engage deeply with the world through his writing and activism. This engagement allowed him to create meaning and leave a lasting impact, demonstrating the power of revolt.

Camus' philosophy of revolt has resonated with many who seek to navigate the challenges of life with integrity and purpose. His ideas encourage us to confront absurdity with courage and to find meaning through our actions and commitments.

NOVEMBER 8: PAUL RICOEUR - HERMENEUTICS OF SUSPICION: CRITICAL APPROACH TO INTERPRETATION

P AUL RICOEUR, A FRENCH philosopher, introduced the concept of the hermeneutics of suspicion, which involves a critical approach to interpreting texts and cultural phenomena. Ricoeur argued that interpretation should go beyond surface meanings to uncover underlying power dynamics, ideologies, and hidden motivations. This approach draws from thinkers like Marx, Nietzsche, and Freud.

Ricoeur used the example of ideology critique to illustrate the hermeneutics of suspicion. He argued that interpreting political texts requires uncovering the power structures and interests that shape them, revealing how language and ideology can manipulate and control. This critical stance allows for a deeper and more insightful understanding of texts.

Ricoeur's hermeneutics of suspicion has influenced literary theory, cultural studies, and philosophy, promoting a more critical and reflective approach to interpretation. His ideas encourage us to question and analyze the deeper meanings and implications of cultural artifacts.

November 9: Paul Ricoeur - Narrative Identity: Self-Understanding through Stories

R ICOEUR ALSO EXPLORED THE concept of narrative identity, which suggests that individuals understand themselves through the stories they tell about their lives. He argued that narrative plays a crucial role in shaping personal identity, as it allows individuals to integrate their experiences into a coherent and meaningful whole.

Ricoeur used the example of autobiographical writing to illustrate narrative identity. He argued that when individuals write their life stories, they construct a narrative that gives meaning and continuity to their experiences. This process of storytelling helps individuals make sense of their past and present, shaping their sense of self.

Ricoeur's concept of narrative identity has influenced psychology, literary studies, and philosophy, highlighting the importance of storytelling in self-understanding. His ideas encourage a more narrative-based approach to exploring identity and personal development.

November 10: Paul Ricoeur - Memory, History, Forgetting: Exploration of Collective Memory

I N HIS WORK "MEMORY, History, Forgetting," Ricoeur examined the interplay between individual memory, collective memory, and historical understanding. He argued that memory and history are intertwined, shaping how societies remember and interpret the past. Ricoeur also explored the role of forgetting, both as a necessary aspect of memory and as a potential source of ethical and political challenges.

Ricoeur used the example of national memory to illustrate this interplay. He argued that collective memory, such as the remembrance of historical events, shapes national identity and influences political actions. At the same time, the selective nature of memory can lead to the marginalization of certain groups and events, highlighting the importance of critical engagement with history.

Ricoeur's exploration of memory, history, and forgetting has influenced historical theory, philosophy, and cultural studies, promoting a deeper understanding of how societies construct and interpret their past. His ideas encourage a more reflective and critical approach to the study of memory and history.

November 11: Donald Davidson - Theory of Meaning: Language as a System of Conventions

D ONALD DAVIDSON, AN AMERICAN philosopher, contributed significantly to the philosophy of language, particularly through his theory of meaning. Davidson argued that language should be understood as a system of conventions that speakers use to communicate. He emphasized the importance of shared understanding and the role of interpretation in achieving effective communication.

Davidson used the example of radical interpretation to illustrate his theory. He argued that understanding a completely foreign language requires identifying the conventions and patterns that speakers use, allowing interpreters to construct meaning from seemingly incomprehensible utterances. This process highlights the role of conventions and shared understanding in language.

Davidson's theory of meaning has influenced linguistics and philosophy of language, promoting a more interactional and interpretive approach to understanding communication. His ideas emphasize the importance of conventions and mutual understanding in achieving meaningful language use.

November 12: Donald Davidson - Anomalous Monism: Mental Events as Physical but Not Law-Governed

D AVIDSON'S CONCEPT OF ANOMALOUS monism addresses the relationship between the mental and the physical. He argued that while mental events are indeed physical events, they cannot be strictly governed by physical laws. This view reconciles the physical nature of mental events with the autonomy and uniqueness of mental phenomena.

Davidson used the example of intentions to illustrate anomalous monism. He argued that intentions, as mental events, have physical correlates in the brain but cannot be fully explained by physical laws alone. This perspective respects the complexity and distinctiveness of mental phenomena while acknowledging their physical basis.

Davidson's anomalous monism has influenced the philosophy of mind, offering a nuanced approach to the mind-body problem. His ideas challenge reductionist views and promote a more integrated understanding of mental and physical events.

NOVEMBER 13: DONALD DAVIDSON - RADICAL INTERPRETATION: UNDERSTANDING OTHERS THROUGH LINGUISTIC BEHAVIOR

D AVIDSON'S CONCEPT OF RADICAL interpretation involves understanding others by interpreting their linguistic behavior, even in the absence of shared language or cultural background. He argued that this process requires identifying patterns and conventions in speech and behavior to construct meaning and achieve mutual understanding.

Davidson used the example of interpreting a foreign language to illustrate radical interpretation. He argued that by observing how speakers use language in various contexts, interpreters can infer meanings and develop a shared understanding, even without prior knowledge of the language. This process highlights the role of interpretation and context in communication.

Davidson's concept of radical interpretation has influenced philosophy of language and cognitive science, emphasizing the importance of interpretation and context in understanding linguistic behavior. His ideas encourage a more dynamic and flexible approach to studying language and communication.

November 14: G.E.M. Anscombe - Intention: Analysis of Human Action

G.E.M. ANSCOMBE, A BRITISH philosopher, made significant contributions to the philosophy of action through her analysis of intention. In her seminal work "Intention," Anscombe explored the nature of intentional actions, arguing that understanding intention is crucial for understanding human behavior. She emphasized the importance of reasons and motives in explaining actions.

Anscombe used the example of a person baking a cake to illustrate intention. She argued that the act of baking a cake is intentional if it is done for a reason, such as preparing for a party. Understanding the intention behind the action requires considering the reasons and motives that guide it, not just the physical movements involved.

Anscombe's analysis of intention has influenced contemporary philosophy of action and ethics, promoting a more nuanced understanding of human behavior. Her ideas highlight the importance of reasons and intentions in explaining and evaluating actions.

November 15: G.E.M. Anscombe - Virtue Ethics: Revival of Aristotelian Ethics

A NSCOMBE PLAYED A PIVOTAL role in the revival of virtue ethics, drawing on the work of Aristotle to emphasize the importance of character and virtues in ethical thinking. She argued that modern moral philosophy had become too focused on rules and consequences, neglecting the role of virtues in moral life.

Anscombe used the example of honesty to illustrate virtue ethics. She argued that being honest is not just about following rules or achieving good outcomes but about cultivating a virtuous character. An honest person acts truthfully because it is part of their character, not because of external rules or consequences.

Anscombe's revival of virtue ethics has influenced contemporary moral philosophy, encouraging a return to character-based approaches to ethics. Her ideas promote a more holistic understanding of morality, focusing on the development of virtuous individuals.

November 16: G.E.M. Anscombe - Critique of Consequentialism: Modern Moral Theory

A NSCOMBE IS ALSO KNOWN for her critique of consequentialism, the ethical theory that judges actions solely by their outcomes. She argued that this approach is flawed because it neglects the importance of intentions, principles, and moral rules. Anscombe believed that ethical evaluation should consider the moral character and intentions behind actions, not just their consequences.

Anscombe used the example of lying to illustrate her critique of consequentialism. She argued that lying is wrong not just because it may lead to bad outcomes but because it violates the principle of honesty and undermines trust. Focusing solely on consequences can justify morally wrong actions if they lead to perceived good outcomes, which Anscombe found problematic.

Anscombe's critique of consequentialism has influenced contemporary ethics, promoting a more principle-based and intention-focused approach to moral evaluation. Her ideas challenge the dominance of consequentialist thinking, encouraging a more comprehensive understanding of morality.

November 17: Fazlur Rahman - Islamic Modernism: Reforming Islam to Align with Modern Values

F AZLUR RAHMAN, A PROMINENT Islamic scholar, advocated for Islamic modernism, seeking to reform Islamic thought and practice to align with contemporary values and challenges. Rahman emphasized the need to reinterpret Islamic teachings in light of modern knowledge and social contexts, promoting a dynamic and progressive understanding of Islam.

Rahman used the example of women's rights to illustrate Islamic modernism. He argued that while traditional interpretations of Islamic texts often restricted women's roles, a modernist approach could reinterpret these texts to support gender equality and empower women. This approach encourages a more inclusive and adaptable understanding of Islamic teachings.

Rahman's advocacy for Islamic modernism has influenced contemporary Islamic thought, promoting a more critical and progressive approach to interpreting religious texts. His ideas encourage Muslims to engage with modern values and knowledge while remaining rooted in their faith.

November 18: Fazlur Rahman - Contextual Interpretation: Understanding Islamic Texts in Context

R AHMAN EMPHASIZED THE IMPORTANCE of contextual interpretation in understanding Islamic texts. He argued that the Quran and Hadith should be interpreted within their historical and social contexts to uncover their true meanings and relevance for contemporary society. This approach contrasts with literalist readings that ignore the complexities of the original context.

Rahman used the example of jihad to illustrate contextual interpretation. He argued that while jihad is often understood as holy war, its original context in the Quran emphasizes struggle and effort in the path of God, which can include non-violent forms of striving for justice and personal improvement. Understanding the context helps clarify the broader and more nuanced meanings of such concepts.

Rahman's emphasis on contextual interpretation has influenced Islamic scholarship, promoting a more nuanced and historically aware approach to understanding religious texts. His ideas encourage a deeper engagement with the context and circumstances in which Islamic teachings were revealed.

November 19: Fazlur Rahman - Education: Emphasis on Critical and Rational Thinking in Islamic Education

R AHMAN WAS A STRONG advocate for reforming Islamic education to emphasize critical and rational thinking. He believed that traditional Islamic education often relied too heavily on rote memorization and conservative interpretations, stifling intellectual growth and critical inquiry. Rahman argued for an educational approach that encourages questioning, critical thinking, and engagement with contemporary knowledge.

Rahman used the example of Islamic jurisprudence (fiqh) to illustrate his educational philosophy. He argued that students should not only learn the rulings of fiqh but also understand the underlying principles and reasoning behind them. This approach fosters a deeper and more analytical understanding of Islamic law, enabling students to apply it more effectively to modern issues.

Rahman's emphasis on critical and rational thinking in Islamic education has influenced educational reforms in Muslim-majority countries, promoting a more dynamic and intellectually engaging approach to religious education. His ideas encourage the development of a more thoughtful and informed Muslim populace.

November 20: Philippa Foot - Virtue Ethics: Emphasis on Moral Character

PHILIPPA FOOT, A BRITISH philosopher, played a pivotal role in the revival of virtue ethics, which emphasizes the importance of moral character and virtues over rules or consequences. Foot argued that ethical behavior arises from cultivating virtues such as courage, honesty, and compassion, which are essential for living a good life.

Foot used the example of courage to illustrate virtue ethics. She argued that a courageous person not only acts bravely in challenging situations but also embodies courage as a stable and reliable trait. This focus on character and virtue contrasts with other ethical theories that prioritize specific actions or outcomes.

Foot's revival of virtue ethics has influenced contemporary moral philosophy, encouraging a more holistic and character-based approach to ethics. Her ideas highlight the importance of personal development and moral integrity in ethical behavior.

November 21: Philippa Foot - Natural Goodness: Basis for Ethical Judgments

F OOT INTRODUCED THE CONCEPT of natural goodness as the basis for ethical judgments, arguing that
moral virtues are rooted in the natural purposes and functions of human beings. She believed that understanding
human nature and its inherent goals provides a foundation
for determining what is good and right.

Foot used the example of human well-being to illustrate
natural goodness. She argued that traits like honesty and
compassion are good because they contribute to human
flourishing and the fulfillment of our natural purposes. This
perspective grounds ethical judgments in an understanding
of human nature and its needs.

Foot's concept of natural goodness has influenced contemporary ethical theory, promoting a more nature-based approach to understanding morality. Her ideas encourage a
deeper exploration of human nature and its role in shaping
ethical behavior.

NOVEMBER 22: PHILIPPA FOOT - DOUBLE EFFECT: MORAL DILEMMAS

F OOT ALSO CONTRIBUTED TO the discussion of moral dilemmas through the principle of double effect, which addresses situations where an action has both good and harmful effects. According to this principle, an action is morally permissible if the harmful effect is not intended and if the good effect outweighs the harm.

Foot used the example of administering pain relief to a terminally ill patient to illustrate the principle of double effect. She argued that giving a high dose of pain medication is permissible if the intention is to alleviate pain, even if it may hasten the patient's death. The key is that the harmful effect is a foreseen but unintended consequence of pursuing a good end.

Foot's work on the principle of double effect has influenced moral philosophy and bioethics, providing a framework for addressing complex moral dilemmas. Her ideas offer guidance for navigating situations where actions have mixed outcomes, emphasizing the importance of intentions and proportionality.

November 23: John Rawls - Justice as Fairness: Principles of Justice

J OHN RAWLS, AN AMERICAN political philosopher, introduced the concept of justice as fairness in his seminal work "A Theory of Justice." Rawls argued that a just society is one in which the principles of justice are chosen under conditions of fairness, ensuring that all individuals have equal opportunities and that inequalities benefit everyone, particularly the least advantaged.

Rawls used the example of the veil of ignorance to illustrate justice as fairness. He proposed that principles of justice should be determined from an original position behind a veil of ignorance, where individuals do not know their place in society. This ensures that the chosen principles are fair and impartial, as no one can design rules to their own advantage.

Rawls' theory of justice as fairness has had a profound impact on political philosophy and ethics, promoting a more equitable and inclusive approach to social justice. His ideas encourage the development of policies that prioritize fairness and equality.

November 24: John Rawls - The Original Position: Hypothetical State for Fair Principles

C ENTRAL TO RAWLS' THEORY of justice is the concept of the original position, a hypothetical state in which individuals choose the principles of justice under a veil of ignorance. This thought experiment ensures that the principles are chosen fairly, without bias or knowledge of one's own social position, wealth, or abilities.

Rawls used the example of economic distribution to illustrate the original position. He argued that individuals in the original position would choose principles that ensure fair distribution of resources, knowing that they could end up in any position in society. This leads to principles that protect the interests of all, particularly the least advantaged.

The original position has become a foundational concept in political philosophy, providing a powerful tool for analyzing and justifying principles of justice. Rawls' ideas encourage a more reflective and impartial approach to thinking about social justice and equality.

November 25: John Rawls - The Difference Principle: Inequalities Justified if They Benefit the Least Advantaged

R AWLS INTRODUCED THE DIFFERENCE principle as part of his theory of justice, which states that social and economic inequalities are justified only if they benefit the least advantaged members of society. This principle aims to ensure that any inequalities contribute to the overall improvement of society and do not disadvantage the most vulnerable.

Rawls used the example of income distribution to illustrate the difference principle. He argued that higher incomes for some are acceptable only if they lead to greater benefits for the poorest, such as through job creation or improved public services. This principle seeks to balance the benefits of inequality with the need for fairness and equity.

The difference principle has influenced discussions on social justice and economic policy, promoting a more equitable approach to addressing inequalities. Rawls' ideas encourage the development of policies that ensure the well-being of the least advantaged while allowing for productive incentives.

NOVEMBER 26: THOMAS KUHN - PARADIGM SHIFTS IN SCIENCE

THOMAS KUHN, AN AMERICAN philosopher of science, introduced the concept of paradigm shifts in his influential work "The Structure of Scientific Revolutions." Kuhn argued that scientific progress occurs through a series of paradigm shifts, where prevailing scientific theories are replaced by new ones that better explain the evidence. These shifts represent radical changes in the underlying assumptions and methodologies of science.

Kuhn used the example of the shift from Newtonian physics to Einstein's theory of relativity to illustrate a paradigm shift. He argued that Einstein's theory provided a new framework that more accurately explained physical phenomena, leading to a fundamental change in how scientists understood the universe.

Kuhn's concept of paradigm shifts has influenced the philosophy of science, challenging the traditional view of scientific progress as a steady, cumulative process. His ideas highlight the dynamic and transformative nature of scientific development.

November 27: Thomas Kuhn - Normal Science: Routine Work within a Paradigm

K UHN ALSO INTRODUCED THE concept of normal science, which refers to the routine work that scientists do within the framework of an established paradigm. During periods of normal science, researchers focus on solving puzzles and refining the existing theories rather than questioning the underlying assumptions. This work solidifies and extends the paradigm, leading to incremental progress.

Kuhn used the example of research in classical mechanics to illustrate normal science. He argued that during the period of normal science, physicists worked on solving specific problems within the Newtonian framework, such as predicting planetary motions, without challenging the basic principles of Newtonian physics.

Kuhn's concept of normal science has influenced the understanding of scientific practice, emphasizing the importance of paradigms in shaping scientific research. His ideas encourage a more nuanced view of how scientific knowledge is developed and maintained.

November 28: Thomas Kuhn - Incommensurability of Scientific Paradigms

K UHN'S CONCEPT OF INCOMMENSURABILITY refers
to the idea that different scientific paradigms are often incompatible and cannot be directly compared. When
a paradigm shift occurs, the new paradigm brings with it a
different set of concepts, methods, and standards that make
it difficult to evaluate using the criteria of the old paradigm.

Kuhn used the example of the shift from Aristotelian to
Newtonian physics to illustrate incommensurability. He argued that the concepts and methods of Newtonian physics
were so different from those of Aristotelian physics that
they could not be directly compared or evaluated by the
same standards.

Kuhn's concept of incommensurability has influenced the
philosophy of science, highlighting the challenges of com-
paring and evaluating different scientific theories. His ideas
encourage a more critical and reflective approach to understanding scientific change and progress.

November 29: Frantz Fanon - Colonialism: Critique of Colonial Oppression

F RANTZ FANON, A MARTINICAN psychiatrist and philosopher, is best known for his critique of colonialism and its dehumanizing effects on both the colonized and the colonizers. In his influential work "The Wretched of the Earth," Fanon explored how colonialism perpetuates systemic violence, exploitation, and psychological oppression.

Fanon used the example of the Algerian War of Independence to illustrate his critique. He argued that colonialism dehumanizes the colonized, leading to profound psychological trauma and a loss of cultural identity. This oppression can only be overcome through a violent struggle for liberation, which reclaims dignity and self-determination for the oppressed.

Fanon's critique of colonialism has influenced postcolonial studies and social theory, highlighting the enduring impacts of colonialism on contemporary societies. His ideas encourage a deeper examination of the legacies of colonialism and the ongoing struggle for justice and liberation.

November 30: Frantz Fanon - Identity: Impact of Colonialism on Personal and Cultural Identity

F ANON ALSO EXPLORED THE impact of colonialism on personal and cultural identity. He argued that colonialism distorts and undermines the identities of the colonized, imposing foreign values and beliefs while devaluing indigenous cultures. This leads to a crisis of identity and self-worth among the colonized.

Fanon used the example of language to illustrate the impact on identity. He argued that the imposition of the colonizer's language erodes the cultural heritage of the colonized, creating a sense of alienation and inferiority. Reclaiming and revitalizing indigenous languages and cultures is essential for restoring a sense of identity and pride.

Fanon's exploration of identity has influenced postcolonial theory and cultural studies, emphasizing the importance of cultural self-determination and resistance to colonial oppression. His ideas encourage a reevaluation of identity and cultural heritage in the context of colonial history.

DECEMBER 1: FRANTZ FANON - VIOLENCE: ROLE OF VIOLENCE IN LIBERATION STRUGGLES

F ANON CONTROVERSIALLY ARGUED THAT violence plays a crucial role in liberation struggles. He believed that colonialism is inherently violent and that the oppressed must use violence to overthrow their oppressors and reclaim their humanity. For Fanon, violence is a necessary and cathartic force that can dismantle the structures of colonial domination.

Fanon used the example of anti-colonial revolutions to illustrate the role of violence. He argued that the violent resistance of colonized people against colonial forces is a legitimate response to systemic oppression. This struggle not only seeks political independence but also restores the dignity and agency of the oppressed.

Fanon's views on violence have sparked significant debate and influenced revolutionary movements worldwide. His ideas challenge conventional notions of non-violence and emphasize the complexities of liberation struggles.

December 2: Gilles Deleuze - Difference and Repetition: Philosophy of Difference

GILLES DELEUZE, A FRENCH philosopher, developed a philosophy of difference, emphasizing the importance of diversity and variation over sameness and identity. In his work "Difference and Repetition," Deleuze argued that traditional philosophy has focused too much on identity and representation, neglecting the dynamic and creative aspects of difference.

Deleuze used the example of biological evolution to illustrate his philosophy. He argued that evolution is driven by variation and difference, with new species and traits emerging through processes of differentiation. This perspective highlights the generative and transformative power of difference in both natural and social phenomena.

Deleuze's philosophy of difference has influenced contemporary philosophy, encouraging a more dynamic and creative approach to understanding reality. His ideas challenge traditional metaphysical concepts and promote a more fluid and process-oriented perspective.

DECEMBER 3: GILLES DELEUZE - ANTI-OEDIPUS: CAPITALISM AND SCHIZOPHRENIA

IN "ANTI-OEDIPUS," CO-AUTHORED WITH Félix Guattari, Deleuze critiqued traditional psychoanalysis and its focus on the Oedipus complex. He argued that psychoanalysis reinforces oppressive social structures by pathologizing desire and reducing it to familial relationships. Instead, Deleuze and Guattari proposed a more expansive and liberated understanding of desire.

Deleuze used the example of capitalism to illustrate his critique. He argued that capitalism channels and constrains desire through structures of production and consumption, creating a "desiring-machine" that perpetuates inequality and exploitation. By breaking free from these constraints, individuals can explore more creative and fulfilling expressions of desire.

Deleuze's critique of psychoanalysis and capitalism has influenced critical theory and political philosophy, offering new insights into the dynamics of desire and social power. His ideas encourage a more emancipatory and transformative approach to understanding human behavior and social structures.

December 4: Gilles Deleuze - Rhizome: Non-Hierarchical Network

DELEUZE INTRODUCED THE CONCEPT of the rhizome to describe a non-hierarchical, interconnected network of ideas and relationships. Unlike traditional hierarchical structures that emphasize linear connections and clear boundaries, a rhizome is decentralized and multidirectional, reflecting the complexity and fluidity of reality.

Deleuze used the example of the internet to illustrate the rhizome. He argued that the internet functions as a rhizomatic network, with information and connections spreading in multiple directions without a central authority. This structure allows for greater diversity, innovation, and adaptability.

Deleuze's concept of the rhizome has influenced contemporary philosophy, cultural studies, and network theory, promoting a more flexible and interconnected understanding of systems and relationships. His ideas challenge traditional hierarchies and encourage more inclusive and dynamic approaches to organizing knowledge and society.

December 5: Michel Foucault - Power/Knowledge: Interconnectedness of Power and Knowledge

MICHEL FOUCAULT, A FRENCH philosopher and social theorist, explored the relationship between power and knowledge, arguing that they are deeply interconnected. Foucault believed that power shapes what is accepted as knowledge and that knowledge, in turn, reinforces power structures. This concept challenges traditional notions of objective knowledge, suggesting that what we know is influenced by who has the power to define knowledge.

Foucault used the example of medical knowledge to illustrate this interconnectedness. He argued that the development of medical knowledge was not just about scientific discovery but also about establishing control over bodies and populations. Medical institutions, with their power to define health and illness, play a key role in regulating social behavior.

Foucault's insights into power and knowledge have influenced fields such as sociology, anthropology, and political science. His ideas encourage us to critically examine how knowledge is produced and whose interests it serves.

December 6: Michel Foucault - Disciplinary Society: Social Control through Institutions

F OUCAULT INTRODUCED THE CONCEPT of a disciplinary society, where social control is maintained through institutions such as schools, prisons, and hospitals. He argued that these institutions use discipline to regulate behavior, instilling norms and expectations that individuals internalize. This form of power is more subtle and pervasive than overt coercion, shaping people's actions and identities.

Foucault used the example of the modern prison system to illustrate disciplinary society. He argued that prisons are designed not just to punish but to reform and control inmates through surveillance, routines, and regulations. This disciplinary power extends beyond prisons, influencing how society manages deviance and normalizes behavior.

Foucault's analysis of disciplinary society has had a profound impact on our understanding of social control and institutional power. His ideas highlight the ways in which power operates through everyday practices and institutions.

December 7: Michel Foucault - Biopolitics: Regulation of Populations

F OUCAULT ALSO EXPLORED THE concept of biopolitics, which refers to the regulation of populations through policies and practices aimed at managing life and health. Biopolitics involves the use of state power to control and optimize the biological aspects of human life, such as birth rates, health, and mortality. This form of power is concerned with the governance of life itself.

Foucault used the example of public health policies to illustrate biopolitics. He argued that measures such as vaccination programs and sanitation regulations are not just about improving health but also about exerting control over populations. These policies reflect the state's interest in maintaining a healthy and productive populace.

Foucault's concept of biopolitics has influenced contemporary discussions on governance, health, and human rights. His ideas encourage us to examine how power operates through the regulation of life and bodies.

DECEMBER 8: HILARY PUTNAM - TWIN EARTH THOUGHT EXPERIMENT: CHALLENGING THEORIES OF MEANING

HILARY PUTNAM, AN AMERICAN philosopher, is known for his Twin Earth thought experiment, which challenges traditional theories of meaning. In this thought experiment, Putnam imagines a planet identical to Earth in every way except that the substance called "water" on Twin Earth has a different chemical composition (XYZ instead of $H2O$). Despite this difference, the inhabitants of both planets use the word "water" to refer to their respective substances.

Putnam used this thought experiment to argue that meaning is not just determined by internal mental states but also by external factors. The term "water" has different meanings on Earth and Twin Earth because of the different chemical compositions, even though the inhabitants are unaware of this difference. This challenges the idea that meanings are solely in the mind.

Putnam's Twin Earth thought experiment has had a significant impact on the philosophy of language, promoting a more externalist view of meaning. His ideas encourage us to consider how context and environment influence our understanding of concepts.

December 9: Hilary Putnam - Internal Realism: Reality Dependent on Conceptual Schemes

PUTNAM ALSO DEVELOPED THE concept of internal realism, which suggests that reality is dependent on our conceptual schemes. According to Putnam, there is no single, objective reality that exists independently of our minds; rather, our understanding of reality is shaped by the concepts and categories we use to interpret the world.

Putnam used the example of scientific theories to illustrate internal realism. He argued that different scientific frameworks can provide equally valid descriptions of the same phenomena, depending on the concepts and assumptions they use. This perspective challenges the notion of a single, objective truth.

Putnam's internal realism has influenced debates in metaphysics and epistemology, promoting a more pluralistic and context-sensitive approach to understanding reality. His ideas encourage us to reflect on how our conceptual frameworks shape our perception of the world.

DECEMBER 10: HILARY PUTNAM - FUNCTIONALISM: MENTAL STATES AS FUNCTIONAL STATES

P UTNAM CONTRIBUTED TO THE philosophy of mind with his theory of functionalism, which posits that mental states are defined by their functional roles rather than their physical composition. According to functionalism, what matters is how mental states interact with each other and with sensory inputs and behavioral outputs, not the specific material they are made of.

Putnam used the example of pain to illustrate functionalism. He argued that pain is defined by its role in causing discomfort and prompting avoidance behavior, regardless of whether it is experienced by a human, an alien, or a computer. This functional perspective allows for a more flexible understanding of mental states.

Putnam's functionalism has influenced cognitive science and artificial intelligence, promoting a more dynamic and interaction-based approach to understanding the mind. His ideas challenge materialist and reductionist views of mental phenomena.

December 11: Noam Chomsky - Universal Grammar: Innate Linguistic Structures in the Human Mind

NOAM CHOMSKY, AN AMERICAN linguist and philosopher, revolutionized the study of language with his theory of universal grammar. Chomsky argued that all human languages share a common underlying structure, which is innate to the human mind. This universal grammar enables humans to acquire language rapidly and efficiently, regardless of the specific language they learn.

Chomsky used the example of children learning language to illustrate universal grammar. He argued that children can acquire complex grammatical rules without explicit instruction, suggesting that they possess an inherent linguistic capability. This challenges the view that language learning is solely a result of environmental factors.

Chomsky's theory of universal grammar has had a profound impact on linguistics, cognitive science, and psychology, promoting a more innate and structured view of language acquisition. His ideas encourage further exploration of the biological foundations of language.

DECEMBER 12: NOAM CHOMSKY - POLITICAL ACTIVISM: CRITIQUE OF POWER STRUCTURES AND PROPAGANDA

C HOMSKY IS ALSO KNOWN for his political activism and critique of power structures and propaganda. He argues that powerful institutions, such as governments and corporations, manipulate public opinion through propaganda and control of the media. This manipulation serves to maintain the status quo and protect elite interests.

Chomsky used the example of media coverage of wars to illustrate his critique. He argued that mainstream media often portrays conflicts in ways that justify and support government actions, while marginalizing dissenting voices. This selective coverage shapes public perception and limits critical debate.

Chomsky's critique of power structures and propaganda has influenced political science, media studies, and activism, promoting a more critical and skeptical approach to information and authority. His ideas encourage individuals to question dominant narratives and seek alternative perspectives.

DECEMBER 13: NOAM CHOMSKY - MANUFACTURING CONSENT: MEDIA MANIPULATION BY POWERFUL INTERESTS

I N "MANUFACTURING CONSENT," CO-AUTHORED with Edward S. Herman, Chomsky explores how media is used to manufacture public consent for policies that benefit powerful interests. He argues that media outlets, influenced by corporate and political pressures, frame news in ways that shape public opinion and support elite agendas.

Chomsky used the example of media coverage of corporate scandals to illustrate manufacturing consent. He argued that media often downplays or ignores issues that could harm corporate interests, while highlighting stories that align with the interests of their advertisers and owners. This selective reporting creates a biased and manipulated view of reality.

Chomsky's analysis in "Manufacturing Consent" has had a significant impact on media studies and journalism, highlighting the need for greater transparency and accountability in the media. His ideas encourage critical engagement with media content and awareness of underlying biases.

DECEMBER 14: SYED HUSSEIN ALATAS - MYTH OF THE LAZY NATIVE: CRITIQUE OF COLONIAL STEREOTYPES

S YED HUSSEIN ALATAS, A Malaysian sociologist and philosopher, challenged colonial stereotypes in his work "The Myth of the Lazy Native." Alatas argued that colonial powers propagated the stereotype of the lazy native to justify their exploitation and domination of indigenous populations. This stereotype served to dehumanize and delegitimize the colonized, portraying them as inherently inferior and in need of colonial rule.

Alatas used the example of British colonial rule in Malaysia to illustrate his critique. He argued that the British portrayed Malays as lazy and indolent to rationalize their economic exploitation and social control. This stereotype ignored the complex social, economic, and cultural factors that influenced the behavior of the colonized.

Alatas' critique of colonial stereotypes has influenced postcolonial studies and social theory, encouraging a more critical and nuanced understanding of colonial narratives. His ideas promote the reevaluation of historical and cultural assumptions about colonized peoples.

December 15: Syed Hussein Alatas - Development: Indigenous Perspectives on Development

A LATAS ALSO EXPLORED THE concept of development from an indigenous perspective, arguing that Western models of development often impose external values and priorities that do not align with local needs and contexts. He advocated for development approaches that are rooted in the cultural, social, and economic realities of indigenous populations.

Alatas used the example of rural development programs to illustrate his perspective. He argued that top-down development initiatives often fail because they ignore the knowledge, traditions, and practices of local communities. Instead, he called for participatory and culturally sensitive approaches that empower indigenous people to define and pursue their own development goals.

Alatas' insights into indigenous perspectives on development have influenced development studies and policy, promoting a more inclusive and context-sensitive approach to economic and social progress. His ideas encourage a reevaluation of development paradigms and greater respect for local knowledge and agency.

December 16: Syed Hussein Alatas - Intellectual Imperialism: Critique of Western Dominance in Knowledge

A LATAS CRITIQUED INTELLECTUAL IMPERIALISM, the dominance of Western knowledge systems and perspectives in academia and intellectual discourse. He argued that this dominance marginalizes and devalues non-Western knowledge traditions, perpetuating a form of intellectual colonization. Alatas called for a more pluralistic and inclusive approach to knowledge production and dissemination.

Alatas used the example of academic curricula to illustrate intellectual imperialism. He argued that many universities in the Global South adopt Western-centric curricula that prioritize Western theories and authors, while neglecting indigenous knowledge and perspectives. This perpetuates a narrow and biased view of knowledge.

Alatas' critique of intellectual imperialism has influenced discussions on decolonizing academia and promoting epistemic justice. His ideas encourage greater recognition and integration of diverse knowledge traditions in education and research.

December 17: Jürgen Habermas - Communicative Action: Rational Communication

J ÜRGEN HABERMAS, A GERMAN philosopher and sociologist, introduced the concept of communicative action, which emphasizes the importance of rational communication in achieving mutual understanding and social coordination. Habermas argued that through communicative action, individuals can engage in dialogue, free from coercion, to reach consensus and resolve conflicts.

Habermas used the example of democratic deliberation to illustrate communicative action. He argued that in a democratic society, citizens should engage in open and rational discussions to reach agreements on public issues. This process relies on the principles of equality, reciprocity, and transparency.

Habermas' concept of communicative action has influenced political theory, ethics, and sociology, promoting a more deliberative and participatory approach to social interaction and decision-making. His ideas encourage the development of more inclusive and rational public discourse.

December 18: Jürgen Habermas - The Public Sphere: Space for Rational Discourse

H ABERMAS ALSO DEVELOPED THE concept of the public sphere, a space where individuals can come together to discuss and debate matters of common interest. He argued that the public sphere is essential for a functioning democracy, as it allows for the free exchange of ideas and the formation of public opinion.

Habermas used the example of coffeehouses in 18th-century Europe to illustrate the public sphere. He argued that these spaces provided a venue for citizens to engage in rational discourse, discuss political issues, and challenge authority. The public sphere facilitates critical debate and democratic participation.

Habermas' concept of the public sphere has influenced discussions on media, communication, and democracy, highlighting the importance of open and inclusive spaces for public discourse. His ideas encourage the protection and expansion of the public sphere in contemporary societies.

December 19: Jürgen Habermas - Deliberative Democracy: Decision-Making through Informed Discussion

Habermas is a leading advocate for deliberative democracy, a model of democracy that emphasizes the role of informed and rational discussion in decision-making. He argued that democratic legitimacy arises from the process of public deliberation, where citizens engage in reasoned debate and reach consensus on collective decisions.

Habermas used the example of citizen assemblies to illustrate deliberative democracy. He argued that bringing together diverse groups of citizens to discuss policy issues can lead to more informed and legitimate decisions. This process relies on principles of inclusivity, equality, and rationality.

Habermas' advocacy for deliberative democracy has influenced contemporary political theory and practice, promoting a more participatory and reasoned approach to governance. His ideas encourage the development of institutions and processes that facilitate informed and inclusive public deliberation.

DECEMBER 20: ALASDAIR MACINTYRE - VIRTUE ETHICS: REVIVING ARISTOTELIAN ETHICS

A LASDAIR MACINTYRE, A SCOTTISH philosopher, played a key role in reviving virtue ethics, drawing on the work of Aristotle to emphasize the importance of moral character and virtues. MacIntyre argued that modern moral philosophy had become too focused on rules and consequences, neglecting the role of virtues in ethical life.

MacIntyre used the example of courage to illustrate virtue ethics. He argued that a courageous person not only acts bravely but also embodies courage as a stable and reliable trait. This focus on character and virtue contrasts with other ethical theories that prioritize specific actions or outcomes.

MacIntyre's revival of virtue ethics has influenced contemporary moral philosophy, encouraging a more holistic and character-based approach to ethics. His ideas highlight the importance of personal development and moral integrity in ethical behavior.

December 21: Alasdair MacIntyre - Tradition: Importance of Historical Context in Ethics

M ACINTYRE EMPHASIZED THE IMPORTANCE of tradition and historical context in understanding ethics. He argued that ethical practices and values are deeply embedded in particular historical and cultural traditions. To understand and evaluate ethical behavior, one must consider the historical narratives and social practices that shape it.

MacIntyre used the example of the Homeric tradition to illustrate the role of tradition in ethics. He argued that the virtues celebrated in Homer's epics, such as honor and loyalty, are rooted in the social and cultural context of ancient Greek society. Understanding this context is essential for appreciating the ethical significance of these virtues.

MacIntyre's emphasis on tradition has influenced contemporary ethical theory, promoting a more context-sensitive approach to understanding morality. His ideas encourage a deeper engagement with the historical and cultural dimensions of ethical life.

December 22: Alasdair MacIntyre - Narrative: Life as a Coherent Story

M ACINTYRE ALSO EXPLORED THE concept of narrative, arguing that individuals understand their lives as coherent stories. He believed that personal identity and moral agency are shaped by the narratives we construct about our lives, integrating our experiences into a meaningful whole.

MacIntyre used the example of autobiography to illustrate the role of narrative. He argued that when individuals write their life stories, they construct a narrative that gives meaning and continuity to their experiences. This process of storytelling helps individuals make sense of their past and present, shaping their sense of self.

MacIntyre's concept of narrative has influenced contemporary philosophy, psychology, and literary studies, highlighting the importance of storytelling in self-understanding and ethical development. His ideas encourage a more narrative-based approach to exploring identity and moral agency.

DECEMBER 23: JEAN BAUDRILLARD - SIMULACRA AND SIMULATION: HYPERREALITY

J EAN BAUDRILLARD, A FRENCH sociologist and philosopher, explored the concept of hyperreality in his work "Simulacra and Simulation." Baudrillard argued that in contemporary society, the distinction between reality and representation has become blurred, leading to a state of hyperreality where simulations and models replace actual reality.

Baudrillard used the example of Disneyland to illustrate hyperreality. He argued that Disneyland is a perfect model of all the entangled orders of simulacra. It is presented as imaginary in order to make us believe that the rest is real, whereas all of Los Angeles and the America surrounding it are no longer real, but belong to the hyperreal order and to the order of simulation.

Baudrillard's concept of hyperreality has influenced post-modern theory, media studies, and cultural criticism, encouraging a more critical examination of the ways in which media and technology shape our perceptions of reality.

December 24: Jean Baudrillard - The Gulf War Did Not Take Place: Media and Reality

I N HIS PROVOCATIVE BOOK "The Gulf War Did Not Take Place," Baudrillard argued that the media's portrayal of the Gulf War created a hyperreal event that obscured the actual war. He claimed that the war was experienced more as a media spectacle than a real conflict, with images and narratives constructed by the media overshadowing the real events.

Baudrillard used the example of televised news coverage to illustrate his point. He argued that the constant stream of images, statistics, and commentary created a version of the war that was disconnected from the actual experiences of those involved. This media representation became the dominant reality for the public.

Baudrillard's analysis of media and reality has influenced media studies and cultural criticism, highlighting the ways in which media can construct and distort our understanding of events.

DECEMBER 25: JEAN BAUDRILLARD - CONSUMER SOCIETY: CRITIQUE OF MODERN CULTURE

B AUDRILLARD ALSO CRITIQUED MODERN consumer society, arguing that consumption has become a central aspect of contemporary life, shaping our identities and social relationships. He believed that consumerism creates a culture where the value of goods is determined not by their utility but by their symbolic meanings and the status they confer.

Baudrillard used the example of luxury goods to illustrate his critique. He argued that people buy expensive items not for their practical use but for the social status and identity they represent. This focus on symbolic consumption leads to a superficial and alienating culture.

Baudrillard's critique of consumer society has influenced cultural studies and sociology, encouraging a deeper examination of the social and psychological impacts of consumerism.

December 26: Jacques Derrida - Deconstruction: Analyzing Texts to Reveal Hidden Meanings

JACQUES DERRIDA, A FRENCH philosopher, is best known for developing the method of deconstruction, which involves critically analyzing texts to reveal hidden meanings and assumptions. Derrida argued that texts are not closed, coherent systems but are instead full of internal contradictions and ambiguities that can be uncovered through careful analysis.

Derrida used the example of literary texts to illustrate deconstruction. He argued that by examining the ways in which texts use language, we can uncover the underlying assumptions and biases that shape their meanings. This process reveals the complexities and instabilities of language and meaning.

Derrida's method of deconstruction has influenced literary theory, philosophy, and cultural studies, promoting a more critical and nuanced approach to interpreting texts.

DECEMBER 27: JACQUES DERRIDA - DIFFÉRANCE: MEANING ARISES FROM DIFFERENCES AND DEFERRAL

D ERRIDA INTRODUCED THE CONCEPT of différance to explain how meaning is created through differences and deferral in language. He argued that words and concepts gain their meanings not through a direct relationship with things but through their differences from other words and their contextual use.

Derrida used the example of language to illustrate différance. He argued that the meaning of a word is always deferred, as it depends on its relationship with other words and the context in which it is used. This deferral creates an endless play of meaning, challenging the idea of fixed, stable meanings.

Derrida's concept of différance has influenced linguistic theory, philosophy, and literary studies, encouraging a more dynamic and relational understanding of meaning and language.

DECEMBER 28: JACQUES DERRIDA - LOGOCENTRISM: CRITIQUE OF WESTERN PHILOSOPHY'S FOCUS ON REASON

DERRIDA CRITIQUED LOGOCENTRISM, THE Western philosophical tradition's emphasis on reason, logos, and fixed meanings. He argued that this focus on rationality and clear definitions overlooks the complexities and ambiguities inherent in language and thought. Derrida believed that deconstructing logocentrism can reveal alternative ways of understanding and interpreting the world.

Derrida used the example of philosophical texts to illustrate logocentrism. He argued that traditional philosophy often prioritizes reason and clarity, marginalizing other forms of knowledge and expression. By deconstructing these texts, we can uncover the limitations and biases of logocentric thinking.

Derrida's critique of logocentrism has influenced contemporary philosophy, encouraging a more pluralistic and open-ended approach to knowledge and interpretation.

December 29: Félix Guattari - Schizoanalysis: Alternative to Psychoanalysis

FÉLIX GUATTARI, A FRENCH psychoanalyst and philosopher, developed schizoanalysis as an alternative to traditional psychoanalysis. Schizoanalysis focuses on the productive and creative aspects of desire, rather than viewing it as something to be controlled or repressed. Guattari argued that desire is a positive force that can drive social change and personal transformation.

Guattari used the example of creative expression to illustrate schizoanalysis. He argued that artistic and cultural production can channel desire in ways that challenge social norms and open up new possibilities for thinking and living. This approach contrasts with traditional psychoanalysis, which often pathologizes desire.

Guattari's schizoanalysis has influenced critical theory, psychology, and cultural studies, promoting a more dynamic and emancipatory understanding of desire and subjectivity.

December 30: Félix Guattari - Ecosophy: Ecology, Technology, and Social Relations

G UATTARI INTRODUCED THE CONCEPT of ecosophy, which integrates ecological, technological, and social perspectives to address contemporary environmental and social issues. He argued that solving these problems requires a holistic approach that considers the interconnectedness of natural, technical, and social systems.

Guattari used the example of sustainable development to illustrate ecosophy. He argued that addressing environmental challenges requires not only technological solutions but also changes in social relations and cultural practices. This integrated approach promotes a more sustainable and equitable future.

Guattari's concept of ecosophy has influenced environmental philosophy and social theory, encouraging a more comprehensive and interdisciplinary approach to understanding and addressing global challenges.

December 31: Félix Guattari - Deterritorialization: Breaking Free from Established Structures

G UATTARI ALSO EXPLORED THE concept of deterritorialization, which involves breaking free from established structures and boundaries to create new spaces and possibilities. Deterritorialization challenges fixed identities and categories, promoting fluidity and transformation in social, cultural, and personal contexts.

Guattari used the example of migration to illustrate deterritorialization. He argued that the movement of people across borders disrupts established social and cultural boundaries, creating new forms of identity and social relations. This process can challenge existing power structures and open up new possibilities for social change.

Guattari's concept of deterritorialization has influenced cultural studies, sociology, and political theory, encouraging a more dynamic and transformative approach to understanding social and cultural phenomena.

Bonus 1: Derrick Bell - Critical Race Theory: Analysis of Race and Law

D ERRICK BELL, AN AMERICAN legal scholar, is a foundational figure in Critical Race Theory (CRT), which analyzes the ways in which race and law intersect to produce and maintain social inequality. Bell argued that racism is embedded in legal systems and structures, and that the law often perpetuates racial injustice rather than eliminating it.

Bell used the example of landmark civil rights cases to illustrate CRT. He argued that even when legal victories are achieved, they often fail to address the deeper, systemic issues of racial inequality. These cases can serve as a means to placate demands for justice without enacting meaningful change.

Bell's work in CRT has influenced legal studies, sociology, and education, promoting a more critical examination of how laws and institutions impact racial dynamics. His ideas encourage ongoing efforts to address and dismantle systemic racism.

Bonus 2: Derrick Bell - Interest Convergence: Racial Progress and White Interests

B ELL INTRODUCED THE CONCEPT of interest convergence, which suggests that significant progress in racial justice occurs only when it aligns with the interests of white people. He argued that advances in civil rights are often granted when they also serve the economic or political interests of the dominant group, rather than out of genuine commitment to equality.

Bell used the example of the desegregation of schools in the United States to illustrate interest convergence. He argued that the Supreme Court's decision in Brown v. Board of Education was influenced by the broader geopolitical context of the Cold War, where racial segregation undermined America's image as a leader of the free world.

Bell's concept of interest convergence has influenced discussions on civil rights and social justice, highlighting the complex interplay between progress and self-interest. His ideas encourage a more nuanced understanding of how and why racial advancements occur.

BONUS 3: DERRICK BELL - STORYTELLING: NARRATIVES TO HIGHLIGHT RACIAL INEQUITIES

B ELL ALSO EMPHASIZED THE importance of story-telling in highlighting racial inequities and challenging dominant narratives. He believed that personal stories and narratives can reveal the lived experiences of marginalized communities, providing a powerful counter to abstract legal and policy debates.

Bell used the example of his own fictional stories, such as "The Space Traders," to illustrate storytelling. In this story, he imagined a scenario where aliens offer the United States economic prosperity in exchange for all African Americans. This allegory highlights the persistent devaluation of Black lives and critiques the notion of progress based solely on economic terms.

Bell's use of storytelling has influenced Critical Race Theory and social activism, emphasizing the power of narrative to expose injustice and inspire change. His ideas encourage the use of diverse voices and stories to enrich the understanding of social issues.

Bonus 4: Richard Rorty - Pragmatism: Truth as What Works in Practice

R ICHARD RORTY, AN AMERICAN philosopher, was a leading figure in the revival of pragmatism. He argued that truth is not an objective correspondence with reality but is instead defined by what works in practice. Rorty believed that philosophical and scientific theories should be evaluated based on their practical consequences and usefulness.

Rorty used the example of scientific progress to illustrate pragmatism. He argued that scientific theories are adopted not because they provide a perfect mirror of reality but because they enable us to predict and control our environment more effectively. This pragmatic approach prioritizes practical outcomes over abstract truths.

Rorty's pragmatism has influenced contemporary philosophy, promoting a more flexible and outcome-oriented approach to knowledge and truth. His ideas encourage a focus on practical implications and real-world applications of theories.

BONUS 5: RICHARD RORTY - ANTI-ESSENTIALISM: REJECTION OF FIXED, INTRINSIC PROPERTIES

RORTY ALSO EMBRACED ANTI-ESSENTIALISM, rejecting the idea that things have fixed, intrinsic properties that define their essence. He argued that concepts and categories are contingent and socially constructed, shaped by historical and cultural contexts rather than reflecting any inherent nature.

Rorty used the example of social roles to illustrate anti-essentialism. He argued that roles such as "teacher" or "leader" do not have fixed essences but are defined by the practices and conventions of specific societies. This perspective challenges the notion of universal, unchanging identities and highlights the fluidity of social constructs.

Rorty's anti-essentialism has influenced philosophy, cultural studies, and social theory, promoting a more contingent and context-sensitive understanding of concepts and identities. His ideas encourage a more open and flexible approach to thinking about social roles and categories.

BONUS 6: RICHARD RORTY - IRONY: AWARENESS OF THE CONTINGENCY OF ONE'S OWN BELIEFS

R ORTY INTRODUCED THE CONCEPT of irony as an awareness of the contingency of one's own beliefs and commitments. He argued that recognizing the historical and cultural contingency of our beliefs can foster a more tolerant and flexible attitude towards others. This ironic perspective encourages openness to change and dialogue.

Rorty used the example of liberal democracy to illustrate irony. He argued that while we can be committed to the values of liberal democracy, we should also recognize that these values are not grounded in any absolute truth but are contingent on our historical context. This awareness can promote humility and openness to alternative perspectives.

Rorty's concept of irony has influenced contemporary philosophy and political theory, encouraging a more reflective and adaptive approach to beliefs and commitments. His ideas highlight the importance of recognizing the contingency of our perspectives.

BONUS 7: DANIEL DENNETT - CONSCIOUSNESS EXPLAINED: SCIENTIFIC APPROACH TO UNDERSTANDING CONSCIOUSNESS

D ANIEL DENNETT, AN AMERICAN philosopher, has made significant contributions to the philosophy of mind and cognitive science. In his book "Consciousness Explained," Dennett presents a scientific approach to understanding consciousness, challenging traditional notions of the mind. He argues that consciousness arises from complex computational processes in the brain rather than from any mysterious or non-physical elements.

Dennett used the example of neural networks to illustrate his point. He explained how patterns of activity in the brain's neural circuits can give rise to conscious experiences, much like how software processes information in a computer. This perspective demystifies consciousness and aligns it with our understanding of physical processes.

Dennett's scientific approach to consciousness has influenced cognitive science, neuroscience, and philosophy, promoting a more empirical and mechanistic view of the mind. His ideas encourage ongoing research into the neural and computational basis of consciousness.

BONUS 8: DANIEL DENNETT - INTENTIONAL STANCE: INTERPRETING BEHAVIOR BY ATTRIBUTING INTENTIONS

D ENNETT ALSO INTRODUCED THE concept of the intentional stance, a strategy for interpreting behavior by attributing intentions, beliefs, and desires to agents. This approach helps us predict and understand the actions of others, whether they are humans, animals, or even machines.

Dennett used the example of playing chess against a computer to illustrate the intentional stance. By attributing intentions such as "the computer wants to capture my queen," we can better anticipate its moves and strategies. This approach is useful even if the computer does not have actual desires or beliefs.

Dennett's intentional stance has influenced philosophy of mind, artificial intelligence, and cognitive science, offering a practical framework for understanding complex behaviors. His ideas highlight the importance of considering intentionality in interpreting and predicting actions.

BONUS 9: DANIEL DENNETT - DARWIN'S DANGEROUS IDEA: EVOLUTION AS A UNIVERSAL ACID AFFECTING ALL AREAS OF THOUGHT

I N "DARWIN'S DANGEROUS IDEA," Dennett explores the profound implications of Darwinian evolution for various fields of thought. He describes evolution as a "universal acid" that dissolves traditional boundaries and reshapes our understanding of life, mind, and culture.

Dennett used the example of biological adaptation to illustrate evolution's wide-ranging impact. He explained how the principles of natural selection apply not only to biological organisms but also to ideas, cultural practices, and technological developments. This perspective emphasizes the adaptive and evolving nature of all complex systems.

Dennett's exploration of Darwinian evolution has influenced evolutionary biology, philosophy, and cultural studies, promoting a more integrative and dynamic view of change and development. His ideas encourage the application of evolutionary principles to diverse areas of inquiry.

Bonus 10: Peter Singer - Animal Liberation: Ethical Treatment of Animals

P ETER SINGER, AN AUSTRALIAN philosopher, is a leading advocate for animal rights and ethical treatment of animals. In his groundbreaking book "Animal Liberation," Singer argues that animals deserve equal consideration of their interests, challenging the traditional view that humans have greater moral worth.

Singer used the example of factory farming to illustrate his argument. He highlighted the intense suffering and poor living conditions of animals in industrial agriculture, calling for a shift towards more humane and ethical treatment. This perspective emphasizes the moral obligation to consider the welfare of all sentient beings.

Singer's advocacy for animal rights has influenced ethical theory, animal welfare, and environmentalism, promoting greater awareness and action towards reducing animal suffering. His ideas encourage a more compassionate and inclusive approach to ethics.

BONUS 11: PETER SINGER - EFFECTIVE ALTRUISM: USING RESOURCES TO DO THE MOST GOOD

S INGER IS ALSO A prominent figure in the effective altruism movement, which advocates for using resources
in ways that maximize positive impact. Effective altruists
prioritize evidence and reason to determine the most effective ways to improve the world, whether through charitable
donations, career choices, or personal actions.

Singer used the example of malaria prevention to illustrate
effective altruism. He argued that donating to organizations
that provide mosquito nets can save lives more cost-effec-
tively than many other charitable initiatives. This approach
emphasizes the importance of evaluating the impact of our
actions to ensure we are doing the most good.

Singer's promotion of effective altruism has influenced
philanthropy, ethics, and social activism, encouraging individuals and organizations to make more informed and
impactful contributions. His ideas highlight the importance
of strategic thinking in addressing global challenges.

BONUS 12: PETER SINGER - UTILITARIANISM: MAXIMIZING WELL-BEING FOR ALL

S INGER IS A STAUNCH advocate of utilitarianism, a moral theory that emphasizes maximizing well-being for the greatest number of beings. Utilitarianism evaluates actions based on their consequences, aiming to produce the most overall happiness and reduce suffering.

Singer used the example of global poverty to illustrate utilitarianism. He argued that affluent individuals have a moral obligation to donate a portion of their income to effective charities, as this can significantly improve the lives of those in extreme poverty. This perspective prioritizes actions that lead to the greatest net positive impact.

Singer's utilitarianism has influenced ethical theory, social policy, and activism, promoting a more consequentialist approach to moral decision-making. His ideas encourage individuals to consider the broader implications of their actions and strive to maximize collective well-being.

Bonus 13: Martha Nussbaum - Capabilities Approach: Focus on What Individuals Can Do and Be

MARTHA NUSSBAUM, AN AMERICAN philosopher, developed the capabilities approach, a framework for assessing human well-being that focuses on what individuals are able to do and be. This approach emphasizes the importance of providing opportunities for people to achieve their potential and lead fulfilling lives.

Nussbaum used the example of education to illustrate the capabilities approach. She argued that access to quality education is essential for individuals to develop their capabilities and pursue their goals. This perspective highlights the need for social policies that support human development and empowerment.

Nussbaum's capabilities approach has influenced social and political theory, development studies, and human rights, promoting a more holistic and inclusive understanding of well-being. Her ideas encourage a focus on expanding opportunities and capabilities for all individuals.

Bonus 14: Martha Nussbaum - Emotions: Role of Emotions in Ethical Life

N USSBAUM HAS ALSO EXPLORED the role of emotions in ethical life, arguing that emotions are not just irrational impulses but are integral to our moral reasoning and ethical decisions. She believes that emotions such as compassion, love, and anger can guide us towards ethical actions and a deeper understanding of justice.

Nussbaum used the example of compassion to illustrate her argument. She explained how compassion involves recognizing and responding to the suffering of others, motivating us to take actions that alleviate pain and promote well-being. This perspective emphasizes the ethical significance of emotional responses.

Nussbaum's exploration of emotions has influenced ethics, psychology, and philosophy, promoting a more nuanced and empathetic approach to moral reasoning. Her ideas highlight the importance of integrating emotions into our understanding of ethics and justice.

BONUS 15: MARTHA NUSSBAUM - GLOBAL JUSTICE: PROMOTING JUSTICE ON A GLOBAL SCALE

N USSBAUM HAS MADE SIGNIFICANT contributions to the discussion of global justice, advocating for principles and policies that promote fairness and equality on a global scale. She argues that addressing global injustices requires a commitment to human rights, international cooperation, and the promotion of capabilities worldwide.

Nussbaum used the example of global health to illustrate her perspective on global justice. She argued that wealthier nations have a moral obligation to support health initiatives in poorer countries, as access to healthcare is a fundamental capability that affects overall well-being. This approach emphasizes the interconnectedness of global justice and human development.

Nussbaum's work on global justice has influenced international relations, human rights, and development studies, encouraging a more equitable and inclusive approach to addressing global challenges. Her ideas promote the pursuit of justice and fairness beyond national borders.

Bonus 16: Kwame Anthony Appiah - Cosmopolitanism: Global Citizenship and Ethical Universalism

K WAME ANTHONY APPIAH, A Ghanaian-British philosopher, is known for his advocacy of cosmopolitanism, which promotes the idea of global citizenship and ethical universalism. Appiah argues that all human beings belong to a single community, and we have moral obligations to each other regardless of national, cultural, or religious differences.

Appiah used the example of global cooperation to illustrate cosmopolitanism. He argued that addressing global challenges such as climate change and poverty requires a sense of shared responsibility and collaboration across borders. This perspective emphasizes the importance of recognizing our interconnectedness and acting in the interest of global well-being.

Appiah's cosmopolitanism has influenced ethics, political philosophy, and international relations, promoting a more inclusive and universal approach to moral and political issues. His ideas encourage a broader perspective on citizenship and ethical responsibility.

BONUS 17: KWAME ANTHONY APPIAH - CULTURAL IDENTITY: FLUID AND MULTIPLE NATURE OF IDENTITIES

A PPIAH ALSO EXPLORES THE fluid and multiple nature of cultural identity, arguing that identities are not fixed or singular but are shaped by various influences and contexts. He believes that recognizing the complexity of identity can lead to greater understanding and respect for diversity.

Appiah used the example of his own multicultural background to illustrate his argument. He explained how his identity is shaped by his Ghanaian, British, and American experiences, reflecting the fluid and dynamic nature of cultural identity. This perspective challenges rigid and essentialist views of identity.

Appiah's exploration of cultural identity has influenced cultural studies, sociology, and anthropology, promoting a more nuanced and flexible understanding of identity. His ideas encourage the acceptance and celebration of diverse and evolving identities.

BONUS 18: KWAME ANTHONY APPIAH - ETHICS: MORAL CONSIDERATIONS IN A GLOBALIZED WORLD

A PPIAH ADDRESSES THE ETHICAL challenges of a globalized world, advocating for moral principles that account for the interconnectedness and diversity of contemporary society. He argues that ethical considerations must go beyond local and national boundaries to address global issues and promote universal values.

Appiah used the example of global trade to illustrate his perspective. He argued that ethical trade practices should consider the impact on workers, communities, and the environment worldwide, not just the interests of individual nations or corporations. This approach emphasizes the importance of global ethical responsibility.

Appiah's work on ethics in a globalized world has influenced international ethics, political philosophy, and global justice, promoting a more comprehensive and inclusive approach to moral decision-making. His ideas highlight the need for ethical principles that address the complexities of global interdependence.

Bonus 19: Judith Butler - Gender Performativity: Gender as Performed Rather than Innate

J UDITH BUTLER, AN AMERICAN philosopher and gender theorist, is known for her theory of gender performativity, which argues that gender is not an innate characteristic but is constructed through repeated actions and behaviors. Butler believes that gender identity is created and reinforced through social performances rather than being a fixed or natural trait.

Butler used the example of everyday actions to illustrate gender performativity. She argued that behaviors such as dress, speech, and body language are performative acts that construct and reinforce gender identity. This perspective challenges traditional views of gender as a biological or essential characteristic.

Butler's theory of gender performativity has influenced gender studies, queer theory, and feminist philosophy, promoting a more fluid and dynamic understanding of gender. Her ideas encourage the questioning of rigid gender norms and the exploration of diverse gender expressions.

Bonus 20: Judith Butler - Heteronormativity: Critique of Norms Surrounding Gender and Sexuality

B UTLER ALSO CRITIQUES HETERONORMATIVITY, the cultural and social norms that privilege heterosexuality and traditional gender roles. She argues that these norms marginalize and oppress those who do not conform to them, reinforcing a binary and restrictive view of gender and sexuality.

Butler used the example of legal and social institutions to illustrate heteronormativity. She argued that laws, policies, and cultural practices often assume and enforce heterosexuality as the norm, excluding and discriminating against LGBTQ+ individuals. This perspective highlights the need for more inclusive and equitable approaches to gender and sexuality.

Butler's critique of heteronormativity has influenced queer theory, sociology, and cultural studies, promoting greater awareness and acceptance of diverse sexual and gender identities. Her ideas encourage the dismantling of oppressive norms and the creation of more inclusive societies.

BONUS 21: JUDITH BUTLER - FLUID AND CONSTRUCTED NATURE OF IDENTITY

B UTLER EMPHASIZES THE FLUID and constructed nature of identity, arguing that identities are not fixed or inherent but are shaped by social, cultural, and political contexts. She believes that recognizing the fluidity of identity can lead to greater freedom and flexibility in how we understand and express ourselves.

Butler used the example of transgender identities to illustrate her argument. She explained how transgender individuals challenge traditional notions of gender by embodying the fluid and constructed nature of identity. This perspective supports the idea that identities can be diverse and evolving.

Butler's exploration of the fluidity of identity has influenced contemporary philosophy, gender studies, and social theory, promoting a more dynamic and inclusive understanding of identity. Her ideas encourage the acceptance of diverse and changing identities.

Bonus 22: Achille Mbembe - Postcolony: Analysis of Post-Colonial African States

A CHILLE MBEMBE, A CAMEROONIAN philosopher, is known for his analysis of post-colonial African states, which he explores in his work "On the Postcolony." Mbembe examines the complexities and contradictions of post-colonial societies, highlighting the ongoing impact of colonialism on political, social, and economic structures.

Mbembe used the example of post-colonial governance to illustrate his analysis. He argued that many African states continue to grapple with the legacies of colonial rule, including issues of corruption, authoritarianism, and economic dependency. This perspective emphasizes the need to understand the historical and structural factors shaping post-colonial societies.

Mbembe's analysis of the postcolony has influenced post-colonial studies, political science, and African studies, promoting a deeper understanding of the challenges and dynamics of post-colonial states. His ideas encourage critical reflection on the legacies of colonialism and the pursuit of more equitable futures.

Bonus 23: Achille Mbembe - Necropolitics: Power Over Life and Death in Contemporary Politics

MBEMBE ALSO EXPLORES THE concept of necropolitics, which examines the ways in which contemporary political power exerts control over life and death. Necropolitics highlights how states and institutions determine who lives and who dies, often through practices of exclusion, violence, and oppression.

Mbembe used the example of conflict zones to illustrate necropolitics. He argued that in areas affected by war and violence, political power is often exercised through the control and destruction of life, creating zones of death and suffering. This perspective challenges traditional views of political power as solely life-affirming.

Mbembe's concept of necropolitics has influenced political theory, sociology, and human rights, encouraging a more critical examination of the ways in which power operates through violence and death. His ideas highlight the need to address the ethical implications of political practices that devalue human life.

Bonus 24: Achille Mbembe - Afropolitanism: Hybrid African Identity in a Global Context

M BEMBE INTRODUCED THE CONCEPT of Afropolitanism, which celebrates the hybrid and cosmopolitan nature of contemporary African identity. Afropolitanism embraces the diverse cultural influences and global connections that shape modern African experiences, challenging narrow and essentialist views of African identity.

Mbembe used the example of African diaspora communities to illustrate Afropolitanism. He argued that these communities exemplify the blending of African and global cultures, creating dynamic and multifaceted identities. This perspective highlights the richness and complexity of African identity in a globalized world.

Mbembe's concept of Afropolitanism has influenced cultural studies, African studies, and diaspora studies, promoting a more inclusive and celebratory understanding of African identity. His ideas encourage the recognition and appreciation of the diverse ways in which African identities are expressed and lived.

Acknowledgements

We extend our deepest gratitude to the countless philosophers whose ideas and writings have shaped this book and helped us review and refine these many chapters. Their contributions to human thought are immeasurable, and it is an honor to bring their wisdom to a wider audience. We also thank our readers for their curiosity and commitment to exploring the rich history and landscape of philosophical inquiry. Your reading and thinking through these pages is a testament to the enduring power of philosophy.

Made in the USA
Columbia, SC
18 November 2024

46818051R00255